The Challenging Sea of an Awoken Heart

Carried by Waves of Destiny

Maria Melo

Copyright © 2025 by Maria Melo
All rights reserved.
No portion of this book may be reproduced in any form without written permission from the publisher or author, except as permitted by U.S. copyright law.

ISBN Paperback: 979-8-9929422-3-1
ISBN Hardback: 979-8-9929422-4-8

Acknowledgements

I start with God, my special friend who has never abandoned me, who has given me the courage and the strength to keep on going, who's voice has guided me through many challenges and struggles during my journey on Earth. Thank you, my dear Jesus, for knowing me better than I do.

My husband Terry, for all you've done to allow me the time to write and for all the meals you cooked while I've navigated through the many lines of these written pages. You are my rock, you are my best friend, and I am so grateful for you my love and my twin flame.

My son, Matthew, my greatest inspiration, I thank you for your support and for your love. Your wisdom is beyond your springs of light on Earth. I couldn't imagine my walk without you, my son. Crystal, my daughter in law, you're always there, and I am grateful for your constant encouragement. Anieta, my dear friend, your love and your help with the editing has been beyond what words could ever say or express; I am filled with a deep appreciation for you. You are a beautiful soul and such gentle and wise lady. I loved working with you and also loved the times we laughed, the times that tears filled our eyes but we both held them back knowing that memories of pain can also help heal, can be the strength and the courage of an amazing life.

To everyone else that has been with me throughout my walk on Earth I'd like to thank you all for challenging my faith and my love, for challenging my demons and my angels, my courage and my fears.

With you all I've learned love above hate, light above all that could keep me lost in emotions that aren't worthy of living for. With you I've learned myself and my power to choose, I've learned to love you regardless of the wrongs done. I thank you all for being part of my life.

May you all be blessed, gods speed throughout your travels on Earth.

Dedication

This book is dedicated to the victims of crime, of violence and of abuse. The people whose rights of speaking up and speaking out have been taking away; whose voices have been silenced by oppressors and by narcissistic systems.

The people of my heart, and the souls of my soul, I know your pain.

Here's a toast to all of you who have passed on to the after-life and to the many people that are still here on Earth working their way through corruption and misconducted societies. Carried out by institutions and leaderships that should be standing for the highest good of humanity, they didn't then and still don't. Power is anger, and anger won't ever be satisfied or lead to the safety of my fellow civilians, nor give back to them what was unjustly taken from them.

I toast to the courage of all civilians, for keeping on going without ever giving up.

I toast to all my spirit friends, my faithful friends, beings of Love and Light that have been with me, walked with me through the darker times and yet never left my side.

May the Saviour our Lord bless you and protect you all.

Long live your hearts of love, of light and of mercy.

Foreword

I have only known Maria for a year or two. We came to know each other through a mutual friend at a time when Maria and Terry were planning to go to the Azores Islands for an extended trip. They needed someone to look after their special cat Zara. Fast forward a year later, Maria and Terry were taking a short trip to the interior, and after their return Maria asked in passing if I can edit, because she's writing a book. I didn't have any experience but I had just observed in myself how sensitive I am to feeling into words and the meaning that they're wanting to bring across. So, I told Maria I would be happy to try it and see.

It became quite clear from the start how well we worked together. I tried doing some editing without having Maria sitting next to me but that did not nearly have the same impact. In fact, it caused confusion for both of us. It was through meeting regularly and reading her written material, paragraph by paragraph, where I could ask her questions and feel into what she was wanting her reader to know. In this meeting of heart and mind I was able to feel into what she wanted to convey. Together we would find a clearer and more expressive way of wording her messages. Even though Maria's mother tongue is Portuguese, she has a good understanding of the English language. With Maria's wisdom and lived experience, and my feeling sense of her meaning and my descriptive ability in English, we managed to find a more elaborate and emotional expression of her messages. We experienced paragraphs and chapters where the words just flowed and jumped onto the pages. In contrast, we also found times and sentences in paragraphs where we struggled to find meaning and the appropriate words to describe the essence of Maria's experience. Once we moved down to Maria's crystal room these opposing experiences only seemed to be amplified even more. Overall, we found the crystals were supporting us greatly in this marriage of hearts and minds to express into words the sometimes-indescribable experiences Maria has had.

Many times, we had laughter and other times I had tears streaming down my face. Maria is strong woman both in her convictions and in her expressions. Despite the hardships she has had to face, her passion for life is quickly felt when in her presence. She is always positive, upbeat and funny. But, when necessary, a fierce use of words can make clear Maria's stance and faith.

It was quite early on in our meetings that I discovered Maria's love for God. She uses those words throughout her book and in her daily expression, but I did not understand the depth of those words. It was in her story telling of events and experiences that I learned how deeply her love for God truly is, and how impactful this love has been in her life to give her the strength she needed in her darkest hours.

Over the course of the months in which we worked together on this auto-biography, it was not without my own emotional and spiritual pains of awakening that I found solace in Maria. She was able to give me guidance to have patience and that great spiritual awakening does not happen without the struggle of learning, nor without the struggle of facing my own shortcomings, faults, and blindness. This required a different level of sensitivity and listening. Maria could read me numerous times to support my emotional torment, physical exhaustion, and lift me up with insights about some of my childhood traumas. It was during these times; I would often find myself lying awake at night. All of a sudden one sleepless night, I found myself praying. Something I wasn't prone to do, and certainly not something I would care to admit to anyone. Clearly Maria's love for God was rubbing off on me, without my conscious knowing. Her faith is genuinely impacting me and it is my true heartfelt wish that you may find some of that imparting on you throughout this book.

God really does love a sense of humour, and if your intention is pure, he really does listen.

Thank you, Maria for trusting me with your message and allowing my input. You truly are a special case ... of love.

Anieta

Looking back, life was full of contradictions. Who knew it would unfold the way it did.

Chapter 1

The Island Life Of Little Maria

My parents were born and raised on one of the Azores islands. An archipelago in the middle of the Atlantic Ocean, they are an autonomous region of Portugal. The islands are characterized by dramatic landscapes, green pastures, and long hedgerows of hydrangeas. Surrounded by the beautiful crystal blues and greens of the salty Atlantic waters. Their rocky coastline with lush green foliage hides many a beautiful waterfall. You'd think I was born in paradise. *Yes, I was!*

Saõ Miguel is the name of the island where my parents were born, and it is the biggest of the nine islands. After my parents got married, they moved away to a different island and started their life journey there. Terceira was the name of this island. These were new beginnings, and both were young and full of dreams, from what they told me when I was still very young.

On Terceira Island they had 6 children, four boys and two girls. Unfortunately, the first two girls and the second boy passed away just a few months after being born. Of course, I never knew these sisters and brother of mine, but I cried while listening to this. I can't imagine the pain my parents carried of having to bury their babies because they couldn't afford medical assistance. I don't even know if this was something that was available in the middle of the Atlantic at that time. I'm also not even aware of the exact dates, but I think this would have been between 1950 and 1958. I remember too, stories of poverty and the difficult conditions of every-day life. The extreme level of poverty still saddens me to this day, such hardships we all had to endure to make life work, even though we lived in this beautiful piece of heaven.

The Azores are located over a triple junction of three large tectonics plates below the ocean: the North American plate, the Eurasian plate and the Asian African plate. They are prone to extreme earthquakes and volcanic activity, and many times devastatingly claimed countless lives.

In 1964 the island of Saõ Jorge was severely damaged by the trembles of Mother Nature. Many of the towns were left in big piles of total debris, a lot of people had perished, and if they did survive, there wasn't much left to return to. So, it happened too that after this earthquake many people evacuated the island. My intuition tells me that it was during this destructive and devastating time that my spirit connected with my parents' minds. Because that's where I was born a few years later.

Terceira island at the time in 1964 wasn't affected by the earthquakes, but it didn't have enough employment for everyone and my dad needed to find a job that could provide better for his family. A high percentage of the population lead the simple life of farming or fishing, owning and working on their plantations. Eventually my father did own his own farm with cows, corn and horse-trade.

The Challenging Sea of an Awoken Heart

A friend of his told him about the catastrophic events that had affected Saõ Jorge Island, and how workers were needed to help with the rebuilding of homes and buildings. For my father this was a ray of hope, as he had to support his young family, so he decided to go to Saõ Jorge Island and try his luck there. He left my mother and my three brothers behind with some of his family members, and boarded the ship to his next destination, saying it would be for two or three months and he would come back for them.

He kept his promise, and three months later he came back to get his family. I remember very clearly my parents telling the story of their arrival on the island. At that time there wasn't the option to travel between the islands by plane, all travel was done by boat.

By its very nature, the Atlantic Ocean was and can be very deceiving. On the Azores islands the winds are always in charge, even on a sunny day. It has the power to alter our plans and help us search for new options. In our family story, my parents arrived late at night with my three elder brothers who were all young children. A hurricane started as soon as they arrived, and they were completely lost in the stormy, dark night. It was pitch black everywhere in the town where they were supposed to be living. The rains were torturous, and the roads had become so muddy that the ground they were walking on became unsteady beneath their feet.

Dad used to say that they were blessed that the strong hurricane winds didn't send them all to heaven that night. The torrential rains had flooded the little basement space that my father had as a home for him, for mom and my three little brothers. They started to knock on doors and ask for help. As I recall these events, I think to myself, God is good, and people can be good too, because, finally, a good Samaritan offered a warm space for them to stay for the night and help them find their way in the morning. That's how Saõ Jorge Island became the island where my parents settled, and they lived there till God called them Home.

The Challenging Sea of an Awoken Heart

Even though they came from another one of the Azores's islands, being new residents of Saõ Jorge Island, they were treated like outsiders, hurtfully being harassed, bullied and made fun of for their accent. Most of Saõ Jorge Island residents didn't really like outsiders, in fact they hated them. Would you call that discrimination? Back then, that was how things went. I don't know what it was. Maybe in today's terms we would call it bullying and discrimination. Neighbourhood kids or classmates would hide in the bushes and attack me on my way home. I would get kicked, punched and slapped. Don't ask me how, I just dealt with it in different ways. And needless to say, some people probably disliked me more than my siblings, but if I couldn't be heard then I had to demand that we be respected just for being fellow neighbours and humans. Needless to say, before I was 11 years old, some of them did learn to respect my family and never mess with me and my little siblings.

I was born there followed by my four sisters; I am the seventh child of eleven children including my siblings who had passed away. I remember many things from my childhood that I wished I didn't. I remember alcoholism and the pain and destruction it caused. It didn't affect each of us the same way but especially my middle and youngest brother, as well as myself, got the worst of it. I certainly won't ever forget the transformation of my father from a noble, caring, and humbled man to someone would turn into a frightening beast when under the influence of alcohol. I remember as well a woman with a great beautiful heart being broken by pain, slowly but surely, being regularly abused, both physically and mentally. As well as the many times when I was 6, 7, and 8 years old and even when I was in my early teens, that I tried to stop father from hurting mom and being picked up like a weightless feather thrown against a wall. Even so, I remember Mom at times wasn't really aware of her actions either, and her punishments towards me could've cause death or paralysis. But it wasn't my time to stand by and do nothing nor to die!

These people were my parents and I loved them, but there were times I hated them as well. However, their best was in truth very poor, and yet all I can say is, it was the best they knew. In reality most people around us were living in a culture that was evolving very slowly. We were poor but there were people even poorer than my family. I believe deep down my parents were good hearted people, kind and loving, they just didn't know how to control their emotions, or the silent pain that screamed and ripped through their insides in cold blood for all the pain that they also had lived through. Unconsciously they were raising us children in the same kind of hellish memory imprint, perhaps the same ignorance and abuse they were raised with. Even as a young child I knew they had had horrible childhoods. Highly likely their lives had been a lot worse than mine growing up. I was very aware even then that that didn't make it right. Looking back now, I can honestly say everything passes and I forgive them all.

My childhood was full of fear, turmoil and dispair, but I had my little sisters to look after and my focus was on keeping them safe so they didn't have to experience the same horrific situations as I did. I stood up in the face of danger because I loved them, because I cared, and because I understood these adults didn't have a clue of what they were doing. My parents were stuck in trauma and pain, in sadness and grief, and I believe they felt lost in their own lives. They couldn't see a single inch past the trauma they lived through and the pain they were causing us. In the end, the more they hurt me, the more they hurt themselves. I find it so sad. I desperately wish it could have been different on that beautiful island. However, I do treasure the memories of all the hugs and the love that we did share many times, as well as the laughs, the horses and trees, and the vibrant oceanic surroundings.

The Challenging Sea of an Awoken Heart

Be kind to you.

When life challenges your faith

when all of your efforts may feel in vain,

When tired of all,

of trying again and again.

Be kind to you,

for eventually all will come to pass,

nothing stays forever same.

Chapter 2

Love, Forgiveness And Gratitude

Does it hurt to remember all those memories? I say it would hurt more not to remember. The physical pain and bruising did heal. I do feel my heart ache when I remember that my parents had such horrible tormented lives. Unfortunately, I and two of my brothers paid a high price. We experienced the most painful events when it came to beatings and abuse. The pain we endured was never our fault; we didn't deserve it. And this is a truth that I will honor as long as I walk the Earth.

For you, dear readers, this is only a little introduction of my autobiography. Please remember forgiveness is the key to freedom. I believed, and continue to believe, that the person who benefits from forgiveness is the one who forgives. I love this word, forgiveness. Forgiveness is freedom. I know this to be true!

It's also true that without my parents I wouldn't be here. I wouldn't have been able to learn my strength, my courage, and my values. All I have learned is because they gave me life. They challenged my faith and my fears. They taught me what they knew, and I learned what I wanted and needed to learn in order to rebuild my broken pieces.

We do have a choice, regardless of our situation. We have our own hearts and minds, plus we now have the right of free speech. What I learned very fast and at a very young age were survival skills. Even though I didn't say much most the time, I always had my eyes open and my awareness sharpened for signs, such as a quick change of body language of those around me. I kept that awareness while learning with each situation and each beating, what I needed to do to stay safe and stay alive.

When I look back, I certainly feel I've made some good decisions, or as close as possible to being good decisions. The lessons were there, it was up to me to learn the best I could, so later on I could teach the best I've learned. Don't get me wrong, I've made my mistakes in life as well. I too carried a lot of angry emotions. But along the way I learned that they weren't mine. I was a victim of beatings and of so many responsibilities at such a young age. I was also held responsible for many household tasks, such as a clean house, clean laundry for ten people, which was all done by hand and hung outside to dry, when we were blessed with a sunshiny day free from the crazy winds that used to blow all the laundry off the line. And I was also accountable for the safety of my little sisters. If for any reason one of them got hurt because I wasn't supervising properly, I'd be disciplined with more beatings. However, I can rightfully say now, I've learned survival skills and I am definitely a survivor! Regardless of what I've lived through, I whole heartedly, in all of it, will always choose to love more and never hate. Being human, and experiencing so many emotions as a spirit in human conditions, is the most difficult and challenging task of a journey on Earth.

Mom and Dad, I love you both. I have forgiven you both. I know you couldn't possibly have hurt me the way you did without hurting yourselves, and it deeply saddens me that you lived through that extreme pain.

I thank you for this beautiful gift you gave me, my life, and I know you both have found heaven and are enjoying each other's company and also the company of Jesus Christ.

This book is full of everything from emotions of pain, sadness, and anger to heartwarming and joyful emotions as well. More precisely, this book contains my immense gratitude. For all I am now is because of where I have been, the people I've lived with, and the people who I've crossed paths with. The ones that only came to my life for a season or two, and the ones who stayed for a chapter or more, but most definitely for the ones who stayed in my life for the entire manuscript. And that's where my immense gratitude comes from. It came from all my experiences and hardships. All these opportunities that gave me the chance to choose to grow or to stay naïve to the knowledge of fear and despair.

My story is real in every detail, and I now know that I couldn't ever be the strong woman I am without everyone that has been in my life, and the many that still are in my life. Thank you everyone.

Through it all, through every episode and phase of life, pieces of my life's unfolding took shape in the chapters you're now reading. This is my story, and I ask everyone, including you reader, to never give up on your dreams. Live not to blame the unfortunate events of your life on the people that gave you life. When I was a child I, unfortunately, didn't have a choice but to live by what was chosen for me. As adults we have a choice in how to live, in our actions and our words. Yet subjected to the rules of society, family, and being judged by others, and that is part of life and the human condition and emotion. I know that the less we blame, the healthier we grow. Yes, I agree, what we lived through does impact our emotions as humans, but no amount of blame is going to heal any situation or any pain.

AS ADULTS' IT IS OUR DUTY TO TAKE FULL RESPONSIBILITY FOR OUR EXISTENCE ON EARTH

Chapter 3

The Voice Was "The Son Of Man"

It was another beautiful day at the end of summer in 2006, and I had reached the end of my day's first working shift. There was still another hour before I had to pick up my children from school. I was tired and decided to lay down on the family room couch to rest for a bit and enjoy the peaceful quiet time before they came home. My rest was abruptly interrupted, much to my surprise.

Suddenly through the silence of my home a deep and strong voice filled up my entire house. The blundering echo extended from wall to wall, and floor to ceiling. It was a strong male's voice which spoke the words, "The voice is the son of man!" It repeated those same words a few times. I was puzzled and didn't really know what to think of it. My first instinct was to look outside through the window. No one was there, not a living soul was outside. I couldn't lie there and pretend it didn't happen, so I went on searching throughout the house. Slowly, step by step, being cautious not to miss anything that could perhaps soothe my inquiring mind. As I entered my son's room, I couldn't help but notice that his computer's black monitor screen had two tiny written white lines. One line stretched across the top and the other dropped vertically down the lefthand side of the screen. The top line spelled out: follow the guidance you have been receiving. The vertical line spelled out: Letters to God.

At first, I thought to myself, nope, I'm not seeing this. This is not real. But no matter how I looked at it, it was there. And I felt myself becoming very emotional. I knew what the message on top of the screen meant. Hands and legs shaking I slowly sat back down on the couch. I felt my heart well up even more. I was feeling on the verge of tears, and yet felt this wave of gratitude and love. Even though I couldn't understand the Letters to God message, I knew that there was a purpose. Deep down I knew I needed to trust and to be patient. That the many visions were calls from the Divine. This was a sign that confirmed that I could no longer set them aside. I could no longer hide. The call was powerful and loud. But I was also feeling overwhelmed, and to a certain extent I basically felt lost and really didn't know what to do next. Where to start? What am I supposed to do?

I made a decision not to stress myself and to just take one step at the time; one day at the time. Over the course of some time, Spirit and I became kind of close friends, you could say. Sometimes I could hear them, others times see them, or feel them, or both. It was, and still is fascinating, and I feel I couldn't live a long enough life here on Earth to fully express my gratitude. I feel so blessed to have this angelic and heavenly family that has come into my life.

Regardless of having two jobs and being a single parent of two children, I was grateful for this amazing spiritual family that filled my life and my tired body with endless love. This feeling of my body of Light was so assuring and filled with meaning. My life shifted radically. It now became even more exciting to get home to my children and at the end of a busy day to finally retreat to my room, my sanctuary. There, and I don't know how to describe it, but channels opened up to divine communication and divine visions. I experienced the most beautiful encounters of love and light, of life and the afterlife. The most beautiful things I've ever lived, I was living it.

I was touched by a love, a kind of love that is everything, that does not exist outside anything. It's an entity that is eternal. An emotion that you and I are not separate. Most of all I felt the deepest gratitude imaginable for the gift of life itself, the most precious miracle of all miracles. Life was on, you could say. I was on my way to beautiful discoveries.

Raised as a catholic, I was always a strong believer of God, but at a young age of around 9 or 10, I began to pull myself away from religion. I understood that God's teachings were of love, and never to be applied to death. Nor should there be a sentence of Hell as punishment.

My vision of humanity and family was one of my own. I struggled to understand what humanity and families called love, as I found these definitions were neither applied nor respected. In my struggle to understand adults who called themselves the righteous ones, I silently questioned their authority. If it was a righteous form of love, why would I have to constantly look for a safe space where I could read or cry and still be safe without being beaten.

My deepest desire as a young girl, as far back as I can remember, was to grow up and be able to speak my truth from my heart without getting into trouble or being punished. As I was a little different as a child; I could hear and see things others could not. And when I told others what I saw, they would tell me that I was dreaming, although I knew my dreams were different than the reality of my awakened mind. So, I stopped sharing what I saw or heard because I didn't feel it was worthy of sharing with people that didn't believe in themselves.

The Challenging Sea of an Awoken Heart

I'd like to share this one prophetic dream that I had around the age of 8 or 9 years old. In my dream I was standing in the front yard appreciating a huge pile of dry wood that magically had appeared. Which made me very happy because dry wood was needed every week to heat up the concrete oven that we used to bake bread for our family of 10 people. Well, interesting! I thought, I have to share this with my mother, because she was really a kind of 'queen' when it came to interpreting the meaning of dreams. However, she couldn't really understand this one, which lead her to speak with Father to find out if he had any plans of going and purchasing more dry wood. Father assured her there were no such plans before the beginning of the new year.

In reality our front yard had a tall wooden pyramid structure with wooden slats nailed horizontally between two of the vertical poles. Father had built it years before. It was used to dry the corn during the winter time. The corn husks would be woven together and placed over the slats side by side to dry.

Several days passed after I had my dream, and we were hit with a big storm. The craziest storm ever! During the night the roofs of some homes were blown away, which left huge destruction, and our pyramid of corn was also destroyed. What a mess! In truth it was very disheartening, because the corn was also used as part of our food for the winter. A lot of work ahead, and a lot of cleaning up to be done!

Our pyramid came down into a large pile of wood and corn all mixed up. But after all the hard work of cleaning and rescuing some of the corn, what was left was the mountain of dry wood. It was exactly the same pile of wood as what I had seen in my dream. I couldn't believe it! This was the first dream that actually came to be true, and manifested for all the family to see.

The Challenging Sea of an Awoken Heart

It will all be okay,

this too, it will pass.

A new morning will rise,

a new day will start,

new opportunities will knock on your door,

new people will come into your life,

and God will smile at you

because you had the courage to trust,

and the faith to just let it be.

The Challenging Sea of an Awoken Heart

Chapter 4

Adeus Minha Terra Natal (Goodbye My Homeland)

I stepped into a whole other world when, in May of 1985, then 18 years old, I married and moved away from my entire family, and all my friends. Even though my family wasn't perfect, it was the hardest separation I had ever experienced. Oddly enough, at the same time it was also a great new beginning in which I was young and filled with dreams. Beautiful innocent dreams. A new beginning in which I was in love with a man who seemed, in my young mind, to be Prince Charming. He was softspoken and handsome, and I was swept off my feet. This was the first time I had fallen in love, a young and innocent love, that I had never experienced before. But no, I was not the "Snow White" that Prince Charming was looking for, and he probably is still looking for her.

The Challenging Sea of an Awoken Heart

My move away from everyone was like climbing a huge mountain while looking for a treasure. Sadly, I can see now, the treasure was always there on Saõ Jorge. I lived on the most beautiful island surrounded by the most incredible crystal blue waters, and other mesmerizing islands. It wasn't until much later that I fully appreciated the simple and beautiful surroundings of my upbringing.

Life was great for a while, but I missed my family every minute of every day. In my heart I carried the deepest desire to sponsor my parents and my young siblings and bring them to British Columbia, Canada, where I now lived. But with every passing day it felt that that dream was falling further and further away from ever manifesting. I couldn't do it alone and I didn't have any support from my new family.

I quickly came to the realization that I was completely alone, that the rest of my journey would be my very own to travel. Devastatingly, my mother became quite sick shortly after I had moved away. This was something I wasn't informed of by my family because I was having trouble with my pregnancy and they didn't want to worry me. When I finally phoned to give them the news of the firstborn granddaughter, my mom's illness had already progressed far enough and she was on death's door. It was crippling news to me, and I felt a wreck. There was so much I needed to tell her, including that I had forgiven her and that I loved her. Not to forget to mention that after my daughter was born, I was planning to visit my mother. I didn't know with what money. I didn't have any money. I had only recently become a landed immigrant and didn't have a job yet. I knew my husband wasn't going to make that easy for me, but his father did end up getting me the airfare. To me it seemed his father was trying to provide for what his son was not providing. And I appreciated his gesture and kindness very much.

In the meantime, while I was waiting for the day of my departure to finally come, my mother passed away. That dreadful call arrived just as I was leaving the house to go to the airport. After which my mother-in-law promptly announced, now that my mother was dead there was no point of me going. To which my father-in-law stepped in and said, she still has her father and she is going to see him. This kindness is something I'll never forget; I will always remember it deep down in my heart with so much appreciation.

Unfortunately, back on the Island of São Jorge, the body of any deceased person was only kept for twenty-four hours, so when I finally arrived my mother was already buried. I can still recall the scent of the fresh soil on her grave, that small lump of soil that was covering the woman who gave me life. She was the one woman I so dearly loved and the one woman that I so desperately needed to hug and hold one more time in my life. My heart was screaming and my soul was hurting in ways I didn't think was possible. Silently my tears ran down my cheeks, landing on her grave and healing her beautiful heart, sending her kisses and telling her we will meet again.

I stayed with my father and four younger sisters and my brother Jamie for about a month. We were all feeling lost without her presence. Although every one of us was grieving in a different way, there was no doubt that the pain of the loss of our mom was present. Whether it was quiet in the house or not, there were many moments where we just looked at each other hoping one of us could say that this wasn't real, that it was only a bad dream and at any moment she would be walking through the door. She never did, and with every passing day I could feel my father's life fading away. He was lost in the pain, the grief of losing the love of his life.

Time with my family passed way too fast and before I knew it, I was again saying goodbye. With my heart drowning, I smiled and tried to be strong, saying to Father and my siblings that I would soon have them come live with me.

A few months passed, I was back in Canada and so glad to be with my baby girl. Just looking at my child gave me courage and strength every minute of my life to never let go. I'd talk to my family on the phone regularly, and as the months passed my sister Lucia got married. Shortly after my father suffered a stroke and couldn't get better. He was hospitalized for a while. I felt a desperate need to talk to him, I needed to tell him to not let go, to not leave us, to not leave me. I called the hospital and a nurse brought him on a wheelchair to the hallway. That's where the only public phone was available to use. He heard my voice and started to cry and on the other end of the line I was crying. I was doing my best for him not to notice it.

"Father", I pleaded, "please don't cry. You will get better and come live with me." His tears were choking him while he spoke: "I am sorry my daughter but, in this life, we won't see each other again." Adding, "Adeus filha Eu te amo", meaning, goodbye daughter, I love you.

And that was it, my father and I, our last goodbye. I was shattered, and a few days after that call he passed away. I knew in my heart that they were together; my mom and my dad were together again. And regardless of how much as I was hurting, I prefer my pain knowing they were together. Their lives were not about me but about them.

I was so distraught, and many times thought while lost in my grief, where is God? I could not understand why my parents had left. I could not understand why God did not hear my many prayers. I was devastated and heartbroken, and my constant dialogue with God was one of many questions but not any answers. Or so I thought.

How could God do this to me and my family? I believed I had always been there for Him. I was angry, and that's when my separation from God began. I decided that I really was going to do it by myself, to stop looking for God where I used to see Him, or feel Him. Was that the right decision? I don't know, but the more I separated myself from God, the more alone I felt. I felt lost, and with it the many questions about my life and my purpose. In the depth of my grief for my parents I lost the sense of my purpose, it was like drowning in the showers of my heart. My feelings were like grains of sand lost on the shores of destiny.

As tears rolled down my cheeks, memories of loss struck deep in my heart, and I covered my mouth to silence my inner screams. The power of grief can destroy human existence very quickly. Grief is an enemy of the soul. Grief and love, they are two different entities, one does not compliment the other. And if we don't pay attention to grief's degrading vibration, we can get lost very quickly. If we are strong enough, we'll be able to find ourselves again, but if we're not, we'll stay lost for a very long time.

Little did I know at that time, but during my most painful experiences I would also learn many more survival and healing skills. Even in this period of deep emotional pain there were many lessons. It was during many dark hours that I found my Light. How was I to know that later on my mother would become my sweet angel? That the scent of her fresh baked bread would fill the air, that her words would play an old song, and that her kiss would arrive with wings during some extremely difficult times of my life.

The Challenging Sea of an Awoken Heart

Sometimes life is just like this,

to feel happy and sad,

to wish that sometimes life could've been a little different,

a little more of the little things that really are everything.

With this, my heart feels that all is worth it,

that all has a divine purpose,

and that, I too am that purpose.

Time is all we have, and all we don't.

Thank you, time, for giving me the opportunity to live

and to experience life at your own pace,

and to love and experience love in your own way.

Chapter 5

My Brother My Heart, We Will Never Be Apart

Many of my dreams did come true. In 1989 I was blessed with another precious child, a baby boy. Also, I was able to bring my two youngest sisters to live with me. They were 10 and 12 years old when my parents died. They arrived January the 10th of 1990, along with my brother Jaime, who made the trip to assure their safe arrival. That was such a happy day for me. My heart was overflowing with joy of having my little sisters with me again. These were my sisters which I had raised, until I had left to come to Canada. I felt as if my cup was half full, and I could drink from it without ever emptying it, because I was in such gratitude. Finally, they were back in my life again, and I wasn't alone anymore.

I started to feel a lot better. My love became a force for my four children, and my sense of existence and purpose were reignited. I even began thinking of being friends with God again.

IT WAS NEVER GOD'S FAULT

The Challenging Sea of an Awoken Heart

Yes, being friends with God again! My heart began to soften as I began to forgive Him for all the things and tragedies that had happened that I could not understand. Everything I had lived and learned had nothing to do with Him. It was fate. As a child, He was my refuge, my safety. I could talk to Him, and I truly loved Jesus. Because deep within my heart I knew Jesus loved children, and He had asked to never hurt a child. Slowly I started to converse with Him again, and I felt my prayers were being heard once more. However, I wasn't aware that my family and I were about to be hit again in a way that would pierce my heart alive and shred my soul.

My life at home was pretty sad most of the time. The beer bottles were my partner's best friends and daily choice. It was what he lived for. It pained me so deeply to have alcohol being part of my life all over again. With it came my abundance of fears, and many other destructive emotions, which I prefer not to mention. Alcoholism really is an illness; it destroys, and it is the wrecking ball of thousands of beautiful families, not to mention the trauma it causes to those innocent family members, and the time it takes to heal. Sometimes life times.

It was July of 1990 and another working day had ended. I was once again looking forward to come home to all the children. Getting home and opening the door I could hear crying, like painful and agonizing crying. I felt as if my heart would jump out of my chest in agony. I was afraid of knowing the answer but asked the question anyway to my sister Eduarda. Through her sobbing and tears, she told me our brother Jamie passed away. I was completely shocked; I was speechless and my body had gone numb. I was as if the ground underneath my feet was shaking. The three of us hugged and cried for I don't know how long.

Once I had some time to myself, my thoughts turned and had a very different tone. The biggest question on my mind was: Is this a joke?

This different tone in my mind and this question that kept creeping up was bothering me. Was I in denial, or was I trying to save me? What was happening? Was this just a dream and shortly we would wake up and this would be going away? This horrible mortifying pain should not be permitted to exist. But it never went away. It was real. Once again, I felt angry at God, and at the world, at the Angels, at everything! Because right there that moment was so empty of everything that was love, and instead filled with everything that was pain.

Jamie had plans to come live with us, to help me with all the kids. He was working hard and saving his money in order to bring that, so he could help us make a new start, a new beginning where peace and love could exist without threats.

Jamie passed away at work. He was working on his tractor on farm lands, his tractor was about to flip over on a part of the field that was very steep. He saw that he couldn't avoid the accident so he jumped out trying to save himself, but horrifyingly, his head hit a rock and to my knowledge he died shortly afterwards. My eldest brother happened to be close by and saw the tractor flip over. He ran to our Jamie but it was too late, his body was still warm, but he had taken his last breath. Jamie was my best friend, my childhood friend and my brother. It was a tremendous loss. A huge piece of my heart was buried the day he passed. He was only twenty-seven years old, and still had his whole life ahead of him. There was so much that he wanted to do, but destiny had different plans.

I honestly felt that I didn't want to live anymore. There really weren't many reasons to live. At the end of the day, it was just another dull day. Like a slow painful way of dying. That was the way I felt at the time and for some time afterwards. Little did I know that his beautiful soul would save me from making the biggest mistake of my life.

I tried hard to understand these painful and testing times, the heartless lessons. What was there for me to learn? It was as if, when I was about to find a balance through the raging waves, another tsunami would try to drown me. I understood that I had no power over anything, and that I was vulnerable and submissive to a power of the universe and a source of something; what I used to call a source of love, but that I no longer believed in. I was completely lost in the darkness of my grief and of my fear. I can guarantee you, it's a lot worse than being extremely poor. My soul was shredded, and every piece of my broken heart had lost its faith.

Nights, days and months, filled with crying, passed me by. I gradually tried to find a way out of that dark hole of sadness and grief. In my mind, I wanted a way out but without too much suffering. I had become blind and numb by sorrow. It was a destructive way of existing, or no way of existing at all. One night, I came up with the perfect plan to put an end to my suffering, and I was relieved. Was I being selfish? I wasn't thinking about the children who needed me oh so much.

By now you readers may understand that Prince Charming was probably lost in the woods looking for the wrong princess. It wasn't me, and he wasn't the one for me anymore. Anyway, I was leaning on my bed pillows, crying and thinking, and designing my miserable plan to perfection. The thought of the end of suffering gave me a slight pleasure, putting a sad smile on my face, bathed by salty tears. As I was lying there, feeding my agony with the end of my misery, I suddenly got a glimpse of this beautiful white light. That Light manifested my brother Jamie. I couldn't believe my eyes! There he was standing by my bedside. He looked exactly the way he looked when he was alive, but with more peace. I could feel his love and care embrace me, like an endless bliss of eternal love. He was loving and caring, and he smiled so warmly at me while moving his head from side to side, as if to say, No! Then, as gently as he appeared, he gently and beautifully vanished into the Light. It left me speechless and stunned. The feeling that followed was like a big hug, an embrace by a divine peace that I will never forget.

Somewhere inside I knew he had come to save me from my own trap. I just needed him to never leave me again. I knew from there on I would never again allow such contemptuous emotions and pain to lead my thoughts and my heart, or my way of living. Life doesn't end even though there is pain. There was still so much for me to live for. My job on this planet was only at the beginning, and I do have a purpose. I needed to remember that if he showed up again, he would probably kick my butt if I didn't get my act together. I truly did have so much to live for, and from that moment on I believed that he was going to help me in every way he could from the life after life.

I know I had to start by healing my heart and my soul, but I had so much anger still, so much unspoken pain, so many hidden tears that I could only allow when I was alone. Yet my time alone was minimal; it consisted of time for a quick sleep because another day was usually just around the corner and just a few hours away with its many demands.

Where do I begin? How do I heal my heart and my soul? What would be the best way? I had the thought to start by searching for the girl I used to be. I was a girl that never gave up. She was overflowing with faith and love for God and all human beings. And I needed to find her again.

IF FORGIVING IS HEALING, LET'S ALL DO IT! WHAT'S THE PURPOSE OF NURTURING SICKNESS

Chapter 6

In Search Of Myself

It was a search for answers. Answers not only for recent events but of so many years of questions. It was the search for life beyond the veil. Life after life. That's what my brother Jamie revealed to me. Most of all, at that time, it was the search for myself. Somehow along the way, I had forgotten my identity, and my soul was clouded by others' expectations and teachings. It was misled by all those who didn't know how to love, how to care, how to hug, and how to understand my frightened and broken heart. Since the beginning of my life, I was forced to take responsibility for others, for their safety, and everything else that was so much larger than my little self.

My adult life felt empty, and I didn't really know where to start re-collecting the fragments of Maria that were left alone and abandoned.

The Challenging Sea of an Awoken Heart

The path of life that I lived was never my own, but a path that served others. It was full of choices that I made to accommodate those who needed me, and choices which commanded my resignation by being pressured under fear of extreme punishments or being reminded that I wasn't good enough. In all honesty, I was feeling full of everything that wasn't myself. All that my life had consisted of and seemed important became meaningless. It was painful to accept.

Understanding and acknowledging this reality was a turning point. I decided to get back to my books and to my passion for reading. I was searching for ways to grow as a person, ways that could bring me to a deeper understanding of myself as a woman, and as a human. I most desperately wanted clarity about my spiritual truth, my soul and my light that for so long had been far away from my divine sight.

My life had been an accumulation of painful events, and now it had become just a pain- filled life. Did I really ever deserve this? I believe not, I never deserved any of it. In fact, no one does. Not a single person on Earth deserves pain and suffering. Unfortunately, before we become aware of this magnificent truth, we have grown so full of anger and the desire to hurt those who have hurt us, that we fail to love our own selves and make different choices. The holding on to anger is so unhealthy, not only to our bodies and our minds, but also to our souls.

It was in my realization that I still had so much to learn, but where do I find the miracles in these tragedies when the sky which I once looked upon and used to see God, were now sad, empty and clouded by layers of anger, and dirtied by tears of sadness and abandonment. My best friend, God, and my true faith, they too had abandoned me, or so I thought.

My first thought was to invite new friends into my life. Friends that would never leave me or judge me, that would love and accept me at my worst and my best. I thought who could be better than the Angels?

And that's where I started. I began by finding books and reading about the Angels, their messages of love and light, and of forgiveness and compassion. At that time, I believed it was the best choice. Today I know it was the right choice. I read about them and about the different religions. I learned about many different Gods and the miracles they performed. Throughout all the stories and all the books, I read it became clear to me that humanity found ways to blame God and deities of eternal love for their own wrong doings and selfish choices. Men and women didn't want to take responsibility; it was easier to blame God, and sadly it is still what most of humanity does to this day.

I came to understand that humanity was great at taking credit when life was good and prosperity was flowing. The land provided more than enough for every living being, yet, when the time came to experience the absence of abundance it was a different story. Perhaps there was a reason behind the lack, maybe the Earth needed the time to recharge its own divine self and her strength, or maybe a friendly reminder, the importance of appreciation, rather than taking things for granted. It really didn't matter which God was in question. Humanity had conditioned itself to blame more and appreciate less, lack of responsibility and of accountability led, and continues to lead, their lifestyles of unhappiness and misery. Absence of appreciation and gratitude unfortunately keeps beautiful people blind.

So, I was faced with a sad realization. In my life, I had done the exact same thing. I had used the exact same criteria and blamed all faults and tragedies of my life on God, and I had forgotten to appreciate the many miracles in my life. Because whether I believed it or not, there was so much to be grateful for as well. I was not at all proud or impressed with some of the choices I had made, or the energy I'd put into them. I was blinded by fear of loss. I did not realize, however, that we don't lose anything, everything is only borrowed for a moment during this walk-through life. Time is borrowed; we don't belong in Time; we belong to Eternity. Well one thing was for sure, I did learn a lot.

This didn't mean, of course, that I didn't have much more to learn. To the contrary, learning about life doesn't stop. It's a long process of the soul evolving in this lower dimension that we reside in, called Earth.

WE CAN NOT CHANGE OTHERS. IT IS THEIR JOB TO CHANGE THEMSELVES

The Challenging Sea of an Awoken Heart

I liked reading about topics of all things divine, such as Angels, deities, spiritual beings, other worlds, the after-life, and other people's near-death experiences. It was like my heart and soul were just absorbing every word I read and filled me up with awe and wonder. I was awakening to the true self of my never-ending divine soul. On one of the many nights of reading about all the divine that my soul and my heart were starving for, and in my heart with a deep desire to forgive all who had hurt me, and everyone who had cheated me, while in the process of laying to rest, I suddenly experienced the visit of a beautiful woman who gently appeared by my bedside. I didn't know how she appeared there, and I was doubting myself whether what I was looking at was truly happening, but there was no doubt about the most profound pure love and peace that I felt in her presence. That moment was divine. I felt a whole-hearted compassion I had not ever experienced before. Her beauty was heavenly, and her silver hair in particular was something that fascinated me. She looked to be in her mid-thirties and her looks were those of incredible beauty. I was mesmerized and couldn't move my eyes away from her. I also had never before experienced that kind of deep peace throughout my body and mind, and most particularly, my heart. She looked at me with such kindness, as if she knew me, as if she could see through me. My intuition sensed that she also knew how I was feeling. Gently she stretched her arm towards me as if to caress my face, but suddenly as she came close to my face, I became scared and pulled away from her reach. In that moment she faded into a beautiful light; a light that also vanished away gracefully and gently.

What just happened? I went from feeling scared to feeling a deep sense of loss. She had disappeared so suddenly. I felt my heart filled with sadness instead. In that moment, I wished she could have stayed a little longer as I had thousands of questions, I wished to ask her. I prayed to see her again, and while I stayed sitting in that feeling on my bed, she didn't appear again. What did remain in the air was this incredible sweet scent of fruits that I've never experienced here on Earth. This was a heavenly rich scent of the purest diverse fruits filling up the air I was breathing in.

I wanted to go back to that feeling of deep, pervasive peacefulness, that pure love that I had never felt before. I continued to sit there and remained relaxed so I could go back to that feeling I had when she had appeared, and to gift my soul a continuation of that memory of the divine magic that just happened. Feeling that immense love was such nourishment to my soul. My heart was bursting with love and gratitude.

Surprise! Later on, I did see her again while on a journey away from home.

But I'll tell you all about it a little later on in this book.

EVERY TIME WE TAKE A BREATH LIFE STARTS AGAIN

Moving on. Yes, I had to move on from the concept of guilt; from the guilt of not being perfect. And from the pain and the resentment that was weighing on my heart. I didn't want to feel any of that! None of it held my highest good at heart. I didn't want to hurt anyone. Pain is horrible, and I had experienced enough of it during many different chapters of my life. No, I didn't want to cause pain, not even if they deserved to be hurt.

I had two younger sisters and two beautiful children, and looking back, I realize I was not my best at all times. But I was the best I knew to be then, which is different than the best of what I know now. It hurt not being able to provide everything they needed. I felt ashamed for not being able to understand everything in the moments I needed to, when my kids and my siblings needed me to understand. I know now I can't be too critical of myself. I also need to remember that I didn't have the knowledge of a fifty-year old when I was only twenty- three, or twenty-four. As it is said throughout ancient times, to truly know the path one must walk the path.

In my family, as in every other family, there were ups and downs. Most of the time, there were more downs than ups! It was difficult to live on one income, as someone's best friend was alcohol, and his family of choice were his friends, and they were all friends of the bottle. Mostly he really didn't like working or holding onto a job for very long. I don't want to complain too much about it. As I've come to understand it, for him the value of life and the concept of responsibility and of providing was very different from mine. I lived to give and care for others, and he lived for the fun of his habits and for receiving. The truth is that it was a constant struggle to keep the peace, to find safety, and to feel safe at home.

It was a struggle to survive the different ways of abuse without losing my sanity. Keeping my cool for the safety of the kids, and making sure that they weren't being exposed to too much of the craziness. It was challenging to also have teenage sisters around, as well as my two young children, and finding a balance of ease and an over-all peaceful understanding among everyone. Actually, most of the time I was burnt out. All of my energy and working efforts went into providing for everyone I loved. I was the sole provider in my family. The little that was left for me wasn't much, but there was enough love to never let me quit, or give up. What I mean is that my fuel gage was always on low, and I was running on a nearly empty tank much of the time.

Many times, I felt my efforts on meeting all their needs weren't sufficient. I didn't have any more to give. At the time I did the best I could, and I provided the best I had with some sacrifice, but never short of love for them all.

There are those days,

that we need to stop everything we're doing,

we need to reflect on life

and it's events in order

not to lose what is beautiful inside of us.

We need to not lose hope, faith and love.

There are those days that we mustn't allow emotions to speak louder than reason,

and reason not to speak louder than love.

The Challenging Sea of an Awoken Heart

Chapter 7

Breaking The Chains Of Abuse And Control

My sisters grew up and moved on with their lives. They were still young but they were gifted with strong minds and strong wills. I am grateful for their courage and for following their hearts and dreams. These qualities were also needed to do their own healing. Even though I raised them for most of their younger and adolescent lives, surviving loss and overcoming the fear they experienced by losing both of our parents in less than a year at such a young age, I knew they needed all the courage they could gather and never lose faith for themselves to do their own healing. Because truly, only they could do their work, with God's grace. Girls I am so proud of you both.

For myself, I finally made it to a position of some financial ease. As I knew I was going to be the only provider for my children, I created the chance to move on, and taking my children with me, they were ten and twelve at the time. Looking for the peace and freedom that was so long overdue, I started a new life and a new journey that was of my own choosing.

It was a time of goodbyes and separation. It was certainly exciting, and at the same time somewhat anxiety provoking. Overall, this was a happy time for me, but the truth is, there was also sadness. Believe me when I say that there are times when it is hard to break something broken. Leaving a relationship of pain, was everything I had ever known.

Finally, I made the decision, and the next chapter of my life would be chosen by me alone, for me and my children, or at least as close as possible to the best I could do and create. I would be the one making the decisions, taking the lead, making sure my children would be loved, safe, and finally sleep in peace. And, oh God, I knew they deserved so more than that.

WHEN ITS BROKEN IT IS BROKEN, BUT WHEN BROKEN IS ALL YOU'VE KNOWN, IT INS'T EASY TO BREAK

The Challenging Sea of an Awoken Heart

As I look back at the many apologies and the flowers that were delivered to me so often after my final decision of leaving that extremely abusive relationship, I realized it didn't mean anything anymore. All the sorrows and the blossoms arrived way too late. There had been many years and plenty of opportunities to make a better life as a family, to have family as a priority, to be there putting the children to bed, to be there for breakfast and to walk them to school. Fourteen years had come and gone and the free partying man and the alcohol had finally won.

The move was on, my children were my strength and my focus, the light of my life and the reason for me to never let go and to never give up. Their unconditional love and true innocence lit me up on even the most exhausting days. It took time for my mind and heart to realize that it was finally safe to go home, safe to sleep in peace and not having to clean up broken dishes or to see the walls full of holes. Some things in life are impossible to process. The cheating was extremely hurtful. The physical and mental abuse are detrimental to live with. No need to be sorry for me! I am a strong woman. If there's anything I've gained from this experience, it's resilience. And still to this day I empower women to speak up, to take back what was taken from them.

Everything teaches something valuable. The hardest lessons teach us the most valuable values. From my own experience I know that if going through hell doesn't make us wish to become a better person, then it is possible we will never find heaven.

It doesn't change the fact that life was still very hard as I had to work two jobs, but with all that came the amazing feeling of freedom and a deep joy for the opportunity to finally be in charge of my destiny. With it came the incredible sense of peace, that it was safe to be alive, and stay alive.

I was blessed to have my children, and the great clients that appreciated my hard work. There was no time for friends or a nurturing social life, however, but that was okay. My children were my priority and that focus kept me steady throughout my doings.

The Challenging Sea of an Awoken Heart

As a promise to myself, I would find a few minutes at the end of each day, mostly late at night, to start to practice my spiritual gifts. I would meditate and say prayers. It didn't take long for channels to a divine world to open up that Divine Light that held me and kept me safe. This Light that touched and nurtured the divine within me.

And the more I practiced, the better I understood myself. And the more I understood myself, the closer I built a relationship with my own soul. The idea that all is one and one is all became a very clear possibility to me.

Time went by quickly; busily but peacefully. I started to understand so much about life, about humanity, about mortality, and about our own bodies of light. I knew that a great learning process was beginning. My time with Spirit was the nourishment for my soul, the nourishment I had longed for, which helped me align with a consciousness much deeper than anything I've ever experienced or learned from anyone before.

The year 2000 rolled around, and with it the fear about the end of the world, or some catastrophic event that could affect humanity and our world. It was THE topic of conversation among people everywhere. But when the clocks struck midnight, all that anxiety subsided, and as we all know, nothing radically changed for many people. Yet, I ask you, how much do we actually know about others, about their struggles and their fate. I say not much at all. And for many of us we don't really know enough of ourselves and our own lives either, nor do we hear the silent screams from the depths of our heart that echo through the ghostly nights with loss and helplessness.

The Challenging Sea of an Awoken Heart

Unfortunately, for my heart, my family and my relatives, it was a time of many endings, of more goodbyes that were never said, and more times of pain ahead. Sadly, one of those endings was just around the corner. We never prepare or think much about possible tragedies; they sneak up on us and plan the years of our lives to come, but don't give us a chance to learn or to know what lies ahead. To know whether it is permitted to live happily and free from the fear of losing the people you love. It does not give an opportunity to speak, to say something, to say hello and say goodbye. And definitely, we're never provided "an address" of where they can be found. But this is part of life. We plan, fill our hearts and minds with dreams, and wish for all kinds of nightly stars we want to reach and hold, and then, Boom! there comes Life, with the biggest smile ever, and changes everything, including all we dreamed of. Regardless, tragedy or not, Life knows better. And most definitely, Life knows no death.

The Challenging Sea of an Awoken Heart

This moment you're taking for granted,

someone is taking their last breath.

This moment you're given a second chance,

someone is given no chance at all.

Make every moment the best one of your life,

hug lots, love much, smile often, and remember to stay in the moment,

for that is where life happens, that is where all begins and never ends.

Chapter 8

Another Goodbye Without A Goodbye

The deep grief of the years before were finally starting to heal. Although time does not heal everything, based on what I was beginning to know and understand of the reality of life after life, the concept of death is not an understanding based on experience, but it's a mental construct that has been learned from someone else that also has not experienced it. Because, belief it or not, the Dead do speak, but in ways that most humans cannot understand. The Dead don't care about gossip or drama, about who's richer or poorer, about who has the bigger house or the bigger yard, or the high-end car; the Dead don't care one-iota about this stuff. So, if one wants to understand the Dead then they need to be ready to let go of these things that for the Dead have no meaning at all in any way.

Other concepts we have been taught are the teachings of loss, fear, and grief, that death is the end. In many cases this leaves people feeling lost for a very long time before they gain the strength to rebuild themselves and learn to live with a void that can never be fulfilled again. Learn to learn the magic of a new beginning. The fact that we arrive with 'a return airfare' gives me strong reason to believe, and support the belief, that Life does go on. Death is not the end of Life; Death is the beginning of a new Life elsewhere.

THEY NEVER TOLD US THAT ONLY BY BEING BORN WE DIE, AND THAT ONLY BY DYING WE WILL BE BORN AGAIN

The Challenging Sea of an Awoken Heart

Humanity devotedly ignored the teachings of God and his promise of eternal life. Life is eternal, and this crystal ball we live in is only a school room, yet it is up to us to learn. We either give energy to emotions of suffering or to a faith that leads us to find the truth of existing here on Earth. There is the possibility of continuing on living in a higher vibrational dimension of light and of love, and a higher frequency of life among the stars, life among eternal Life. Where Life never ends. Could the truth of life-after-life be a belief? Anyone can believe what they may, however, I prefer a truth that helps me heal my heart. A truth that leads me to help heal others' pain. A truth that gives me strength to endure with love and faith the many obstacles along the path of my life, which was never easy.

I understand being human is the hardest job a being is ever faced with. As a human we are energy in motion, or in other words, emotions. One emotion will call for another emotion. Either positive or negative, whatever we give energy to will lead the show. And sadly, emotions are subject to the creative drama-mind that constantly looks for something to be worried or unhappy about.

No, I didn't know all of this then, and that's okay. I am just like everyone else; a little gift box slowly unwrapping and discovering the different pieces of my soul's many lives and its memories. Who I am, and who we all are, is pure love trapped in teachings of fear. All of it is filled with beliefs of limitations during this confinement in Time.

By July of that year, another painful occurrence took place. The phone rang again with distant devastating news. My sister Lucia's husband had tragically passed away in a motorcycle accident. He was thirty-seven years old and had a six-year-old son. It was heart-breaking, but deep down in my heart, I knew he wasn't gone. He had just returned Home. But how could I tell her that he was Home and safe with the Lord? I didn't know how to help her in a way that she wouldn't hurt so deeply. She was in so much pain and her grief was so real. I desperately wanted to help her, to love her in the ways that I could, but she lived so far away on Saõ Jorge Island. I knew her beautiful soul was feeling lost, probably not knowing what to do with her own existence. There were no words I could say to truly comfort her. I could not hug her close to my heart and hold her during her profound time of loss, pain and grief.

Lucia and I had grown up very close, basically like twins, as we were close in age too. We were best friends at all times. She was my little tiny saint, like an angel on my shoulder, keeping me safe when we were kids. Like, for instance, when I was attempting to ride a horse that had not yet been fully trained, or from doing other dangerous things, Lucia would protect my fearless and adventurous soul while it was taking physical risks.

Lucia was, and still is, tiny in stature, a mini girl, so to speak, and at times in her magical loving mind and heart. As a child she always tried to save injured animals, or look for shelter for them during stormy weather. Now it was her that needed protection, love and support. More than ever before. Her loss shook the ground she stood upon. Her love, her husband, her best friend, her reality was filled with sorrow and uncertainty.

The Challenging Sea of an Awoken Heart

Some time had passed before I received a phone call from a relative back home saying that Lucia had had an accident; her car had flipped over in front of the cemetery where her husband was buried. I was assured that she was okay, but deep down inside my heart I knew she was dying slowly. The fear of losing her invaded my heart. I felt it was best that she should move closer to me and to her other two sisters. I suggested to her to move to British Columbia, which she refused. I understood it was not an easy decision for her. Her family home, the house she had built brick by brick with her husband, the giggles and the dreams, life as she knew it, as well as all her special places would be left behind. It took her some time, but she did eventually come to understand that the memories would be with her forever. And finally, two years later, after her husband's passing, Lucia arrived with her eight-year-old son. It was a very happy day for me. For all of us, my other two sisters and myself, our hearts were overflowing with joy of having her and her young son come live with us. We were filled with gratitude.

NOTHING LASTS FOREVER NOT EVEN OUR PAIN

I felt so relieved. Finally, we were all together again. United by tragedy, but most of all by love and by strength. During our losses we had become the strength for each other. Each one of us had hurt so much, cried at different times, and in different places, and many times the pain of one would be the strength of the other. Love is a miracle and only love sets us free.

After her arrival we started the process of her legalization in Canada. This was a hellish experience that I can never forget. From legal advisors to immigration lawyers, it was a money sucking process, misguided information to all kinds of dead-ends with nowhere to go, except being left behind with an empty bank account. I found out that as a Canadian-citizen I could not sponsor her or her son. After spending thousands of dollars, basically all the funds she had were gone without any firm solution. Tons of money was spent on lawyers, only to be told we had no way of keeping her here legally with us, meaning my other two sisters and I. I remember like it was yesterday, the lawyer saying to me, "get your sister on an airplane and get her out of here". Disappointing to say the least! That was after all the lies and false promises, but he knew we didn't have any more money.

I was told many times that God doesn't sleep. God never sleeps, I now know. Miracles do happen when pure love comes into unity of hearts. God takes the lead. His love knows no end, and this time too He sent us an angel to help with this situation. A miracle occurred which resonated through our lives. We will forever be grateful for this particular angel, and every other divine being who stepped in to help during this very challenging period. To all of you, you know who you are, my most grateful thank you!

Now everything was starting to take shape. The huge and long-lasting stress was finally gone. We could see the light at the end of the tunnel and the path of opportunities, the freedom for choices had opened up for us, but most importantly, opened up for Lucia, and to her son. God is good, oh so good!

BELIEVING IN UNITY, NEVER GIVING UP IS WHAT KEEPS US GOING

The Challenging Sea of an Awoken Heart

Life passes by way too fast! Regardless of all the demands and obligations, we must make the time to prioritize, even though sometimes the priorities are different than the goals we had in mind. Many people are blessed enough with the time to accommodate both. However, that wasn't so in my case, but I was very blessed with what I had.

After years of working two jobs and running around the clock, I realized I had accomplished so much, but sadly I had missed so much with my children while they were growing up. Life had so many demands all the time, especially when it came to finances, meeting the needs of all the expenses of life while providing for my family's daily needs. All of a sudden, I found myself seeing my babies were no longer little, and this reality filled me with an emptiness. I realized I had missed such a large part of their young lives. I couldn't take that, and I tried to push that feeling away. I could never go back. I had provided them with what I believed was everything they needed; I loved them fast, fed them fast, including the time to rest, everything was constantly in the fast lane. My life was always on hyper-speed.

My son was then fifteen years old and my daughter almost eighteen years old, and I was feeling extremely tired. It had been so many years of 14 to 15-hour work days, and that was weighing heavy on me and the family altogether. I've missed so much of what should have been the most beautiful part of my life.

I AM SORRY THAT I DID NOT KNOW ANY BETTER

Chapter 9

De Volta A Casa (Back At Home)

It was 2004 and I planned a trip to the Azores Portugal; a trip back home. I had not been back to Saõ Jorge for about 10 years and I wanted to introduce my children to the place where I was born and raised, including the small house in which once upon a time ten people lived. I wanted to show them the small island and my little town, and to share with them memories of myself as a young girl riding horses and chasing the winds. I remember with the utmost of fondness, the faster the horses ran the better I felt; my soul had wings in those moments. And many times, I wished those times and that excitement would go on forever. It was an exhilarating feeling; the magic of the moment and a freedom I can never forget.

The Challenging Sea of an Awoken Heart

Many memories arose within me as we made plans for our trip. Emotions that had been stored away for so long were trying to creep up on me. That beautiful island held my every root, memories, laughs and as well so much suffering. Something that children shouldn't ever have to experience. I missed my brother and my parents tremendously. Stubborn tears filled my eyes and I so wished my parents were still alive so that they could meet my children. I wish I could hug them and hold them close to my heart, I wish I could tell them I had forgiven them, which I did, and still do every day of my life. But that wasn't the case, they were really gone and I needed to dismiss the wishful thinking out of my aching mind and heart.

Finally plans for the holidays were put together. Not exactly the way I wanted, but to avoid names and to avoid any complications, I will not elaborate any further.

The voyage still happened, and I and my son left July 1st in 2004. It was a bittersweet time. Half of my heart I was leaving behind, and the other half I was taking with me. Matthew, now fifteen years old, was a happy and as always, a good boy. I will never forget how, as the plane was taking off, he held my hand and said, "Thank you Mom!" I looked over, and in his beautiful green eyes was a profound amusement. We began to gain altitude and the clouds started to get closer and closer as the land disappeared farther and farther away. We had about eleven hours left flying on those large wings across the beautiful heavenly skies.

As we approached the Islands, the vision of the beautiful Atlantic Ocean brought memories. Memories of watching it from inside the window at home during wild storms and long winter seasons as the huge waves were crushing upon the shore and hugging the island's highest cliffs. There were times they had claimed lives and land, and took them to the depths of their mother sea, only for the waters to appear crystal clear blue the next morning, like nothing had ever happened. Or to reassure that everything was under divine control, and only He, the universal God, the One in charge of such beautiful creation and mystery could understand the depth of it all.

OUR SOUL'S HOME IS WHERE OUR TINY LITTLE HUMAN LIVES BEGIN

Our arrival was emotional. It had been about 10 years since I visited my relatives the previous time. My middle sister and two older brothers were at the airport. I remember my older brother looking straight at me, and he just kept on looking. He didn't recognize me. When I called his name, he looked me right in my eyes and said: "ohhh, it's you!" And with tears in our eyes, we hugged. Altogether, it was a special meeting, one in which I realized some things never have and will never change. These were my siblings, and even though I didn't know them very well, and never really had a close relationship with these two men, I sure loved them. My heart felt full holding my sister in my arms, even though I had had the chance to see her two years prior as she had visited us in B.C. The grounds of Saõ Jorge that I knew so well nurtured my roots, and that too, would never change.

I was so very happy to be there with my siblings, nephews and nieces, and enjoy them in my daily life for that very special short time. They also loved meeting my son Matthew, and being with him. There was so much love, and even though my brother Jamie and my parents had gone to heaven, they were inside our hearts. I felt indebted that we had each other, and certainly in such deep appreciation to know that my loved ones were really not gone but had just taken a trip back home, a different Home where Life never ends, and where we all will meet again.

WE ONLY DIE WHEN WE ARE FORGOTTEN

The Challenging Sea of an Awoken Heart

The first few days were busy with catching up, talking and laughing, at times until two or three in the morning. To wake up to the roosters singing around five AM took me back again in time to when I was a young girl. I remember that when the roosters sang, Dad would get up and soon after would wake up the rest of us. There was a time that the idea of sedating my dad or the roosters for another two or three hours felt like just the right thing to do! It definitely would've been great to sleep a little longer. Haha, sorry my readers, yes, by nature I do have some interesting thoughts at times, which most of the time does benefit everyone. However, this time I certainly appreciated them singing every morning. I would get up to make sure I wouldn't miss the next few songs. Then more than ever before I really appreciated the beauty of everything, the unity of all with all. Every breath of life. Shortly after 5 in the morning, I would sit outside with my cup of coffee, looking at the beautiful ocean and the two islands across the sea. The air was filled with a scent of farmland and salty waters, a sweet and sour mist, something forever missed. It brought tears to my eyes. I didn't know why I was crying, but possibly for all the ones who had passed over. Or maybe it was for me, or for everything that I wanted to keep in my arms but was too far from my reach. The tears flooded uncontrollably for a while, I was glad everyone else was still asleep, and only this tiny land and endless sea was awake to keep me company.

A little later I could hear the neighbourhood dogs barking and the early farmers driving or riding their horses to their farms. Another busy day was starting for everyone; milking the cows was usually the first task to be undertaken. So much had changed, there were a lot more wheels on the road since I had left the island, but I was happy that there were still horses. Those beautiful animals had always captivated my heart. To me they seemed like beautiful beasts with gentle souls. They fascinated me, and still do.

Many of the people in town did not recognize me, which wasn't surprising as many of them were also very young when I had emigrated. People change with time, and I had changed as well. However, I had in my heart the wish of visiting two elder ladies that I had never forgotten.

The Challenging Sea of an Awoken Heart

When I was very young and was washing by hand the laundry of ten people every day for many years, they would come over and help me, especially when some pieces of the laundry were much larger than my tiny hands. The demand of the workload expected from an eight, nine, ten-, or eleven-years old child was most of the time larger than my tiny body and heavier than my physical strength. But I always tried very hard to accomplish my chores. Whenever I could, especially Thursdays, I would sneak out to the library. I loved reading; it was my sanity and my escape. Reading helped me understand what my parents and my family didn't understand. It helped me feel safe even in the middle of turmoil and chaos. With reading I always ran the risk of being punished, but my passion suppressed my fears. To me I was willing to take the risk of a price to pay, because it kept me outside the bars of constricting conditions of small thinking and of a small island's inhabitants' little imagination.

So, I went and visited those two special ladies, Fatima and Lurdes, who were by then practically housebound, as they were elderly and not well. They had remained living in the same houses, just as I remembered from my childhood. It was so very sweet to see them. They loved visiting with me as much I loved visiting with them. We sat down having tea, speaking of the old days. I told them how much I really did appreciate all the help when I was a very young girl with all that laundry that was bigger than me. The meeting felt like a blessing of some sort. It was kind of like something that was way overdue, like a bill that needed to be paid with a graceful thank you. The fascinating fact is that I knew that if my parents didn't give me all of those chores, then I wouldn't have all of the knowledge and the survival skills that I do now. Even the compassion I carry inside my heart, that too would be a lot different.

Everything teaches something valuable, something money cannot buy because it doesn't sell anywhere! Something we cannot learn in universities, or college, because they don't teach it there. They aren't familiar with these kinds of journeys, and more often than not, teachers of these types of lessons, they don't speak of it. Many are ashamed of their past, and of their relatives. Many of them are trying to fill a void in their lives with empty profiles. And that's okay, I can respect that, but it isn't me. I am my own self. As long I live, I am my story, and my parents have done a lot of unhappy things, but I need to remember that they were likely extremely unhappy. There were times of oppression during their lives and living conditions. They didn't know any better or anything of a better life. But I did learn better, therefore, it is my duty to do better, to be better. And regardless of everything, I am grateful for having had such parents, for they gave me life. This is who I am. Who I am now is because of a culmination of life experiences. In order to be better, I needed to learn better, not forgetting that without them I wouldn't have had this chance of life and to be living here and now. I'm doing my best at sharing with you all that I am perfectly fine with being me, with all my imperfections, and I believe that you as well should be okay with being your beautiful you in your own unique way.

WE DON'T HAVE A CHOICE WHEN WE ARE CHILDREN BUT WE DO WHEN WE BECOME ADULTS

The Challenging Sea of an Awoken Heart

The little house that once was home to my parents and eight children, was now all renovated inside and out, the rock on top of rock was nicely secured by concrete and with a nice finish all throughout the outside. As I walked by it, I couldn't take my eyes off of it. Yes, many changes had happened, but a long and powerful history lay in it, inside their leaking walls and ceilings. The table that sometimes was empty, the tears that never got out the door to speak, to express, or to ask for help. The alcohol that manifested in a diabolic monster, the fears of a woman, her pain and her struggles to survive. She was my mother. Some people say only survivors tell the story. Well, I am one of them. The journey from being a full house to the last resident, its departure- my brother, when he passed away way too young. Everything happened within a very short time, and the painful fatality that separated all of us for the remainder of our lives. I am sure that loss deeply affected all of us in ways that are not completely clear to any of us, but certainly changed the connections that from then to now helps live life in a deeper gratitude and the awareness not to miss celebrating life before death arrives, so that everyone can be present and enjoy the party from outside the box. Only some of my siblings speak of it, others not so much.

My son really wanted to see the inside of the house, or at least have a closer feeling to the place I knew so well. It was where half of his roots lay; his ancestors. My son had never met my parents, but he had seen them in spirit, as they manifested to him when he was ten years old. Since then, he grew very close to his grandfather's memory of love, my dad's soul.

I spoke to my brother Jose about the possibility of Matthew seeing the house inside. Jose said he knew the owners and would speak to them regarding a possible visit to the house. A couple of days later we were informed that the owner was a childhood friend and would love us to visit our childhood home. After twenty years it was an emotional experience. Inside, it was so nicely renovated, nicely divided, warmer and altogether a better house than when I lived there while growing up, but with every step, I knew where everything used to be. As we walked through it, I explained to my son how everything was before. The window where mom used to sit down and sew, or the many times she looked through it hoping to see dad getting home, hoping to see my brothers getting home during days of extreme storms while working on the farms. I knew where every smile was, every tear, every worry and every terror.

The ceilings were now much stronger and properly restored. As a child, during long, stormy nights, with extreme high strong wind, I used to look up at the ceiling and could hear the roof tiles being blown away. The extremely heavy rains finding their way to leak inside the house. The thunder was so loud, it would scare the heck out of me. To this day, I don't like it. During the nights of cyclones, I could hear my mother praying and asking for Saint Barbara and Saint Jerome to ease off the storms. It was comforting hearing her, and silently I would pray with her, her voice was so full of faith, and I was sure that the saints and God would have no choice but to listen to her prayers.

It was a great visit. So much was recalled, and there was so much to be thankful for.

In that house, my life history from six to eighteen years old had played out. It was there that I also learned to protect the innocent. My awareness for angry people and their trapped emotions became very heightened. The way they looked, the way they walked, the way they moved, I learned very quickly that when they would take a step, I was better off taking two. Their angry behaviour and expressions would freeze my spine, but never my feet. It sure was a beyond believe journey, and I was thankful for all that it was. In that moment, being back in that house and looking back on my early years, I felt grateful for all the things and events that helped me grow and choose to better myself. I was not given that choice back then, or at least it was not something that I was free to use, but definitely something that I could put up on a shelf of my subconscious mind and unknowingly place within a possible reach for when I finally could claim the freedom that was mine by birthright.

NOT EVERYTHING IS A CHOICE, SOMETIMES DESTINY CLAIMS PRIORITY

The Challenging Sea of an Awoken Heart

So much was being done during this visit to my homeland. I had this one special thing on my mind for quite some time, which was visiting the house where I was born. This first house was very small, and very old, built on top of a very steep hill. It wasn't far from our second family home, but when I'd lived in the area, I'd never had the desire of seeing it closely ever again. With arrangements, it was possible to revisit the first six years of my life.

That home was different and held less memories. Actually, only a couple of them and they were very vague. One memory in particular left an imprint on me, and it was when I was five years old. Upon seeing the window facing down the hill this memory popped into my mind, and I was being transported back in time. It was during a very stormy day, thunder and heavy rains were washing away parts of some roads, the lightening crashed down and lit up our town and its grounds and fields. It was as if the world around us became a vastness of water and of powerful striking energy. In my young age it felt like the end of the world, being surrounded with water and fire. Before the storm started, mom had gone to the farm to feed some of the animals and left me, my brother Jamie and my sister Lucia at home. We were all very young, three- five and eight years old. When the storm had started, we got so scared and we started to cry leaning against that window that was facing down the hill. Crying and calling for mom to come home. I'm unable to recall for how long, but I can never forget seeing her as she turned that corner of the house and came running home. She was soaked through and wet to her bones. Still, she had that look on her face, as if she was saying, don't worry mommy is back now. As far I can remember that moment was the happiest time at my five years of age, to have mom safely home with us again.

I remember real life stories, some sad and some of them happy. I remember mom saying that I got very sick at the age of three or four years old. She said the doctors did not know what was wrong, but that they believed I was going to die. I fell into a deep sleep for three or four days burning with a very high fever. Mom and dad had done all they could and there was nothing else that they could possibly do, so they prepared themselves for the worse.

FOUR DAYS HAD PASSED

NIGHT AND DAY, A SILENT CRY

THE LITTLE GIRL HAD GONE TO SLEEP

AND NO ONE KNEW EXACTLY WHY

(Excerpt from "The Four-Day Sleep" from Letters to God – my first book)

The Challenging Sea of an Awoken Heart

Together they prepared my only cute dress and my one pair of Sunday shoes, my only shoes to tell you the truth, to dress me up for my heavenly trip. My poor mom.... I can't imagine her pain. But it wasn't my time, and it has become clear during the challenges of my life why death didn't take me then. I woke up after being in a coma for three or four days and just came back to life like nothing had happened, and the fever was all gone. My mother believed it was a miracle, or that the many prayers were answered by messengers of Love and Light. I will say now that I am pretty grateful to be here still, and hopefully when I cross-over I can become an entity filled with goodness and a great sense of humour.

I would come to discover more much later on in life, when I was back in Canada and had just birthed my second child, shortly after which I experienced a very bad cold and cough. It left me feeling like I had two hearts beating inside my chest. When I told this to my doctor, she smiled at me and said that was impossible. I had to convince her to hear it for herself, she said, "I'll check it if it brings you peace to make sure your heart is good." So, she checked, and checked, and checked again. Then she called in the other doctors in the office to check me as well. They all agreed there was something wrong with my heart. Boy did that make me happy! Haha. I said, "see I wasn't lying!" It was almost worth having a heart problem, to prove them wrong! Of course, I'm laughing now, but it's not funny. Although the memory of it is kind of funny. They sent me across the street to another medical office to have a cardiogram done. A short time later I came back with the results to see my doctor. She organized for me to be seen by a heart specialist, who then sent me for an ultrasound. There they discovered I'd had rheumatic fever as a child, had gone into a coma which resulted in the left valve shrinking and leaking. But after all this, I can assure you that I have a great heart, and I have a happy heart. A heart that loves to love! And as long as it continues to beat for me, I'll try to not disappoint it. I still live with this, but I talk to my heart and I tell it how grateful I am for keeping me here on this side of the veil. The mystery was solved and I had been given a second chance. In my heart, I now know I was sent back for a reason, to love and to lead others to love.

The Challenging Sea of an Awoken Heart

Every day that passed by during this trip home was a very rewarding experience, and the healing of everything was a peaceful bliss, filled with an understanding I didn't know I had. I felt compassion for everyone, for all my family past and present. Most of all I felt compassion for myself as I vividly remembered so many sad episodes of my life. As I came face-to-face with my memories, those memories that I thought would only be completely healed the day I would come to pass, they instead came to dissolve by love and forgiveness. No more pain was connected to any of my memories. I could smile and say, it's okay, I understand that you didn't know how to do better, and I still love you. Thank you for all the great and amazing life lessons, that to this day give me the opportunities to choose my heart over conflicted minds.

My son Matthew was enjoying his holidays and the many festivities in different towns. He was free and safe to be a kid and to be happy. However, the few last days I was fully aware that I would be leaving again, and it made me sad. The truth is, I felt as if my life was happening always in a fast lane; running to different sides of the earth, as if to meet myself in the other place, either Canada or São Jorge. As much as I felt I needed to be in both places, in all honesty, I felt I didn't belong anywhere. Even though it seemed I had everything, I knew there was always something missing. It wasn't completely clear but it seemed like a longing to remember something I had forgotten. Was it a soul commitment or was it my agreement with God?

The thought of leaving again filled my heart with sadness, especially when it came to leaving my sister. A piece of my heart and a ray of my sun was staying behind and my heart was in pain. But that was the reality and I needed to be strong. On the other side of the earth, a huge and very important piece of my heart was waiting for me. My daughter, my girl, my child, love of my life.

On our second-to-last day before our departure, we all gathered at a little beach where the children played and swam. The adults barbecued, talked and laughed, trying to keep the goodbyes as sweet as possible. The scenery from that little beach was beyond words, endless beauty merging heavens with earth, all was and is divinely connected. The crystalline Atlantic waters of a heavenly blue, the volcanic black rocks of the mountains behind us held knowledge that we probably would need to live a few more lifetimes to fully understand the minimum of its depth. The beautiful little plants growing from volcanic soil and ashes held messages of love, of faith, and of courage, and in my heart, I silently promised to be back if only to just say hello. It was magical, its energy was filled with whispers of eternal love. It was all part of my existence, my family, my love for God, and my history.

Before I knew it memories were calling me back into the farm fields, the sense of freedom, and the fresh air. I remembered the baby calves, feeding them, holding a bucket with milk under their chins and using my fingers as a soother so they could learn to drink. I always felt fascinated with their angelic beauty. I remember too our family dog, Pastor. His love and protection were always present. I remember the pigs we used to raise and the many times they'd jumped out of their confinement, damaging the garden and all the vegetables, and how upset Mom would be watching her hard work being uprooted. She used to call Dad for help with getting the pigs back into the corral, and Dad would call Pastor, telling him to chase the pigs back. The dog would run, barking, and it sure didn't take long before the pigs jumped back into the corral just as easy as they had jumped out.

These memories were comical, and from there on, any time the pigs jumped out, all Mom and I had to do was to call Pastor, telling him to chase the pigs back. Believe it or not, when the pigs heard the dog's name they wouldn't wait to be chased, they would just run home as quickly as they had run away. Stunning how intelligent pigs are. I love it. Not all memories held sadness, in fact some were filled with true joy and opportunities to learn our magic over and over again.

I had flashes of memories that took me back to when I was about twelve years old. Dad called me outside to go look at something. Excitedly I ran out to him to find a new gorgeous young horse he had purchased. I felt as if my head had wings, and I couldn't wait to take the horse for a ride. As if Dad was reading my thoughts, he said: "Maria, don't ride the horse yet. He isn't fully tamed." Sadly, I relented, but shortly after, Mother asked me to go get something she needed from the grocery store. "Yes Mom," I replied.

When I was leaving to do my chore, I had to walk by the horse. I stopped and admired his beauty and his peace, thinking wow, it would be way faster to the grocery store on the horse. Besides, it really looked like no harm could come from such beautiful, peaceful beast. So, looking around, making sure no one was watching me, I mounted. The trip to the store was at an awesome, nice pace and there were no surprises.

Yes, I was super happy. After getting the couple of things that Mom needed, I started my way back. With the handles of the plastic bag around my left wrist, I started my riding trip back home. As I neared the house, a bit of wind shook the plastic bag scaring the horse and causing him to take off like he had seen the afterlife dressed in black. I was petrified and scared for my life. It didn't matter how much I tried; I couldn't stop him.

I remember seeing couple of shadows outside my house, but I couldn't see who it was and I couldn't wave goodbye, because if I let go, I'd probably fall off the horse. I couldn't wave a sign for help and I didn't have flares with me either…haha. I was certain that day I'd probably die, if not by falling off the horse it would be by punishment. A very sharp turn was just ahead, and I knew that turn very well, leading to a gravel dirt road, and I believed I was going to die there.

As the horse was wildly turning, I jumped off into a huge bush of berries and whatever other thorny bushes were there. I don't remember much of anything after that except rolling into the road. By the time I collected my where-abouts and was getting the awareness of all the aches and pains in my body, my parents were already there, along with a couple of my sisters. I felt dizzy and unbalanced. If anything, I was kind of happy that I could feel something and to actually see them. Even knowing there would be a price for my disobedience, I felt grateful that

The Challenging Sea of an Awoken Heart

I lovingly got checked for broken bones. Anyway, I was happy to be alive! Oh yeah, and the horse, he was nowhere to be seen.

Mom's groceries were not in good condition, and I was in a rough state of being. Physically, mentally, even spiritually. I thought that even my soul had probably exited my body, leaving me by myself with my poor choice. Good for it. I'd probably would've done the same if I was my soul!

Good news, I must say, I didn't get a punishment. My family in truth looked concerned and kind of treated me the way I deserved to be treated, regardless of being disobedient. My body was bruised and sore, so I felt grateful for the opportunity to heal without any further pain or damage. Wow, what an adventure!

This was not the only exciting moment between myself and some of the local animals. There was a time when the pigs we were raising had been moved a little farther down the road, the same road where I had lost the horse. That road became very popular for me. One day close to the evening, my mother asked me to carry some food for the pigs, which I honestly didn't like to do. Carrying the big containers filled with food was extremely heavy. On this particular evening, when my brother Jamie wasn't home, I realized the tractor was parked at the door, and with that awareness a brilliant idea came to mind. Maria, I thought, check to see if the key for the tractor was in the ignition! The key was, indeed, in the ignition, and I stood there trying to recall all the sticks and buttons my brother used to make that beast move. Putting the food bins inside the container attached to the tractor, I checked around for my mom. She wasn't outside or by the windows, so I happily started the tractor and put it in reverse to get out of the driveway. Wow! Quite proudly, I backed up like a pro! I was on my way to feed the pigs their dinner. A couple of minutes after, I heard someone screaming my name. A fast glimpse around and behind me, I saw my mother running after me, or honestly, maybe after the tractor. Ooooh my Jesus, I thought, she doesn't look happy. I could've given her a ride, but I didn't think that would change her angry that she was spewing out of her eyes towards me, or the amount of trouble I was in. Reaching my destination, I wasn't sure if it was safe to stop, she was still running and certainly getting closer to me. I wished the tractor could go faster, but that thing was like a turtle. I decided to stop, and Mom caught up, gasping for air after the wild run. I thought I should just go ahead and feed the animals while she regrouped her strength for the punishment that was coming my way. While I was dragging the pigs' food out of the box, she seated herself on a rock on the side of the road and not far away from the tractor. She was fuming and growling between her teeth. I knew she was going to kill me and probably chew me up too with those sharp teeth. A chill come over me; I wasn't ready to die! I certainly preferred the excitement of chasing death for a little longer. Actually, I don't think Jesus wanted me up there yet.

When I was finished my duty and brought out the empty bins, I put them back inside the little tractor trailer. Mom was now standing, ready for something. She was now eerily calm. I politely asked her if she wanted to learn to drive the tractor. I don't really know if I was trying to break the ice or reignite the fire. She didn't reply. She just growled and gave me a dark stare. The truth is I felt as if my heart could jump out my chest anytime, but I couldn't and wouldn't ever again show any signs of fear. She told me to drive it back home but very slowly. So, I did! As slow as possible. The drive back was actually a little pleasant, to be honest. We somehow engaged in a friendly conversation. I was still scared, and I knew that things could change very suddenly, but nobody was chasing me. When we reached the driveway, I gave her the key and offered to go to the fountain and bring some water home. She seemed happy with that. Again, I survived another exciting and agonizing adventure. I thought as long I was working, I'd probably be safe, so I just kept myself busy. At the end of the day, I cleaned up after everyone's dinner, and when mom had gone to bed, I knew for sure that that episode had become part of the past. It was now part of my history.

Back in the present moment of being on the beach with my family and watching my son, my brothers and sister, nieces and nephews having fun, with my eyes semi-closed, I was feeling extremely sad that this beautiful get-together was taking place just before another goodbye, another separation. However, I also felt a deep sense of gratitude for everyone and everything, knowing we would be leaving again the next day. Another page in the book of my life was being left behind and a new chapter was about to start.

The departure quickly arrived with kisses, hugs, tears and goodbyes. Leaving the islands and beautiful Saõ Jorge Island was difficult. I had discovered a new-found part of my heart, a deeper understanding of love and of compassion, and, most of all, an appreciation for all that had enriched my life, including myself. I felt gratitude too, for a God that I had no clue I was about to start searching for.

The flight back was exciting and I couldn't wait to see all of my girls and all the little ones. Being back, where everything I had created and built was waiting for me, was exciting. They were all at the airport with happy faces and happy smiles. I felt so blessed and loved by all of them. This was home. A faraway land but that's were my soul found the freedom and the strength to learn to fly.

GOD, MORE THAN EVER BEFORE I NEED YOU NOW

The Challenging Sea of an Awoken Heart

Chapter 10

Tragedy, My Son, The Rays Of My Sun

It was now August 13, 2004, and five days had passed since I was back from the amazing and very healing trip. It was a Friday and my heart was feeling tight inside my chest. I felt it was like a phantom pain, something I couldn't understand. A couple of nights prior, I had had a dream that I was walking through an empty warehouse, except for a few large burlap bags. These bags were full and tied at the top. Walking through the area past these bags, I was cautious and did not touch them. As I was standing there for just a moment, I felt uneasy and nauseous. Reluctantly, I decided to open one of the bags to see what was inside. I was horrified as I found a boy inside. A young boy around fourteen or fifteen years old. He was alive. At that moment I woke up, shaking with intense fear at the realization that the other bags probably contained trapped living human beings. I was trembling, and very nervous, but had to remind myself that it was a dream. However, knowing my dreams, maybe it was not just a dream, because since I was a child many of my dreams eventually came to manifest in real life, and they were never pleasant or brought good news. My heart was heavy, silently screaming, and I didn't know what to do about it.

Every Friday, Matthew would stay with the other adult. He would usually pick him up Fridays late afternoon and bring him back next day before or around noon time. That day Matthew was outside skateboarding and playing with his friends, when the other adult drove in to pick him up. As I was looking out the window, Matthew quickly opened the front door sliding his skateboard inside and saying, "Bye mom, I love you". That sound, his voice echoed inside my screaming heart, and as I ran to the door trying to catch up to him, but I was too late. I wanted to give him a hug, and a kiss, but all I saw was the truck driving away with my boy. My heart wanted him back. God, I shouted, what's going on? Why was I feeling a phantom agony? God didn't reply and the best I could do was try to dismiss those agonizing feelings and stay positive. The day seemed to pass by uneventfully somehow and around ten thirty that night I decided to call Matthew to find out what it was that the two of them were doing. He replied they were at home watching a movie. He was safe, so I reassured myself that all was fine, and finally I fell asleep.

Was I dreaming? A heavy knocking on my front door woke me and my sister up. My sister and her son were living with me at the time. Feeling confused and a little lost, I looked at the clock. It was around 3.45 AM in the morning. At the door stood two police officers. The sight of them paralyzed me, and I could not speak. One of them asked me if I had a son by the name of Matthew.

"Yes," I replied, adding, "please tell me my son is okay!" I could see the officer was having a hard time speaking as he explained, "your son is alive, but very badly burned and in very critical condition in Royal Columbian Hospital." He added that the house where Matthew was staying had been set on fire. l burst into tears. My body was shaking and

I felt my heart go into shock; it was pounding faster than I could keep track of. I wasn't able to think and was having a very hard time articulating words. I thanked the officers before closing the door. I told myself over and over, this isn't real. It cannot be real. Unfortunately, it was real. A painful reality that changed my life forever.

Without thinking, as if on automatic pilot, I was trying to change out of my pajamas to normal clothes. I just wanted to get to him as soon as possible. The drive to the hospital felt like forever, and the dark of the night was as sad as my tears. My heart had never experienced so much fear. Pray, cry, scream, just do something! This is what I told myself over and over, as I was so filled with fear of what I was about to witness. My heart was screaming inside my chest. It hurt!

As I arrived through the emergency doors at Royal Columbian Hospital, I felt I was going to faint. Fear was my worst enemy; I was afraid of fear, so terribly afraid. Two nurses walked towards me like they knew me, or were expecting me. I asked to see my son, and they replied by asking if his name was Matthew? "Yes," I said. My voice was as soft as a faint murmur, and I followed them to a badly burnt child. My son, lying there in that bed, intubated and on life support. It's impossible to write what I felt, no words or letters can express what I was feeling. And that smell of burnt skin, it's so hard to describe, that was lingering in the air around my sweet baby, lying helpless in that hospital bed. I can still recall that pungent smell.

I just stood there and cried, looking at that beautiful boy, who just few hours before was a happy and normal boy. "God," I asked, "please save my baby. Can you help my baby?" I couldn't even imagine the pain he had gone through, and the thought of his pain was eating me alive. I was choking on my silent grief. He was so badly burnt. In the bed beside him was the adult he was staying with, also burnt, but not nearly as bad. Around 6.30AM in the morning Children's Hospital sent an ambulance with all the equipment needed to transport my son to his new home. I followed the ambulance, promising that I wouldn't ever leave him alone. I would never leave his side. I would never give up. I would be his strength, his courage, and his eyes. I would do everything possible and impossible to help him. I would find a way to let him know that I was there with him at all times.

As I arrived at Children's Hospital, I had to wait for a few hours without seeing him as doctors and nurses were diagnosing him and getting him set up in the room. Every minute of waiting was filled with indescribable fear, anxiety. and with unanswered questions. They set him up in the ICU, his new home. It was a horrific and painful reality I had never imagined before, and a reality I would never ever wish for anyone.

A few hours later one of my sisters arrived. We just looked at each other, we didn't have any words. We hugged and unstoppable silent tears rolled down our faces. I knew she was devastated, like they all were, and I understood they wanted to comfort me. My pain was agonizing. Speaking at that point wasn't an option. I couldn't talk. I walked a few feet away from her, leaning on the outside hospital wall, and covering my face with my hands. I cried for a long time. I needed and wanted my son back in my arms.

Forty five percent of Matthew's body was covered with third degree burns, and he was in extreme critical condition. No doctor could tell me whether or not he would make it. A chair beside his bed became my bed, and the ICU waiting room became my home. Time had stopped for me. Every monotonous step I took down the hospital hallway filled the emptiness inside with deeper sadness. My existence had turned instantly into a cloud of pain, and my life felt as if I was a ghost. I felt more than empty inside. As if I no longer was existing. Life had robbed me and my boy of the right to happiness.

The two adult brothers who were also burnt were in different hospitals. Sometime later on I came to find out that the fire was caused by arson. Matthew had been sleeping on the living room couch when three cocktail fire bombs were tossed through the living room window, landing on him while he slept. As Matthew was being burned alive, he woke up screaming in pain. He started running, calling the two guys in the house, at that point the living room was all in flames. Matthew was fighting through the flames while burning alive, going down the stairs screaming for one of the adult men. Then both ran towards the third floor to wake up the other adult. Finally, the two adults and my son made it out alive.

A few days later one of the officers came by the hospital to check on Matthew, and shared with me that Matthew had given him his mother's information and that he had not only fought for his own life, but he had saved the other two people. His last words before he was intubated onto life support were: "I could not leave them there to die." And he didn't! From that point on, Matthew started the long battle for his life, a journey of struggle, of pain, of survival, of hate and love, and of forgiveness. His courage, his heart. He is and forever will be my precious soldier of love, of courage, and of strength.

Living pain and breathing pain, still, I couldn't give myself the luxury of thinking of my pain. My true pain was the knowledge of his pain, the pain of his uncertain future, if there was going to be one available to him.

The days were slow and with every second that came along I hoped a doctor would come to me with miracle news that they could save my son's life. But that was my wish. I dreamt of those words, but they were never spoken. On life support, Matthew went from burnt to unrecognizable, due to all the fluids that tripled his body's size. It was a painful scene to watch, but I knew that a powerful soul was beneath that burnt skin, and I made sure that he knew every day that he was so loved and never alone.

Two weeks passed before a doctor finally came and asked to talk to me. He said he didn't know if they could save Matthew's life, but that they would have to do skin graft surgeries. He was holding papers that needed my signature to proceed with surgeries. I asked will it save his life, and he replied that Matthew could die any second during surgery, but that he would surely die if he didn't get any surgeries. My trembling hands held those papers while I was trying hard not to cry. I asked where to sign. There's no way my son would die without me trying everything available to save him and keep him alive.

From there on many hours of long surgeries began. My time was by his side, waiting for a sign of life from him. I talked to him, I told him over and over again how much I loved him and asked him to come back. At times I could see his eyeballs moving below his eye lids to the sound of my voice. I knew he was aware of my voice and I needed to keep his subconscious awake and alive. Matthew loved music. Pink Floyd was his favorite so I went and purchased every CD I could find. I played them over and over again for him. I could see his eyes responding. There was rapid eyeball movement when the music was playing. And I was there beside him, sometimes crying and other times praying, to the rhythm of every song, desperately hoping he would open his beautiful green eyes and look at me.

Life at the ICU wasn't just one of pain, fear and grief. I soon understood that it was a meeting place for the many people who were transitioning onto a path of faith, a path of finding courage that most of us, including myself, didn't know we had. A path where nightmares were real and everyone lived them without even falling asleep. The suffering there was real suffering, and I know how it feels, but I wasn't alone. Rich and poor, all gathered there. Not everyone spoke with an accent but everyone cried and hugged the same way.

One of the early mornings I was coming back from my son's room to the waiting room. A woman was sitting there, crying uncontrollably, her pain I thought was the mirror of my own. My soul felt the urgency to try and soothe her pain, somehow to help her. Quietly I sat down in the space where there was only the sound of her sobbing along with my silent tears. About a half hour passed I didn't move or leave. I didn't want her to be all alone. Finally, she lifted her head up and realized someone else was there with her.

Looking at me, she said, I am very sorry I couldn't help it. I softly responded, "I understand." When the cry is loud, the pain is deep.

The Challenging Sea of an Awoken Heart

Crying, I then said to her, my name is Maria, what's yours? She replied her name was Sandy. We shared a big caring hug. It was the beginning of a one-season relationship, and of an amazing learning experience filled with tears, fear, faith, and a love that helped us help each other. It's true, the quote that says real queens fix each other's crowns. Yes, they do! No matter what they're going through, they are always there for each other.

Sandy's son was born with extreme special needs, and like my boy, he too was 15 years old. Just like my son, his name was also Matthew. All of Sandy's son's life he had been fed through feeding tubes, and he was having many complications breathing. We got to spend some time together, and learned so much about each other's lives. We came to know so much of each other's routines. Every morning, returning to the waiting room, if she wasn't there, I knew she would be sitting next to her son in the ICU. I would sit and visit with them and feel so deeply touched by the love that this mother and son shared. Her precious son looked at her lovingly, and with his smile saying everything that words could never express or speak.

At the same time, in a different corner of the ICU room, my son began his surgeries. The first one was a series of skin grafts on his upper back. Skin was to be removed from his stomach and applied to his back. At first, I felt it was the beginning of a miracle, but when I saw the painful reality not much had changed, if anything it was even more unbearable to see. His back filled with staples and his stomach strapped of skin, all was a bloody painful vision. There was no room for my discomfort however, I needed to be strong. I needed to not cry around him. I also asked family and friends who visited not to cry or make sounds of lamentations, as I knew he could hear a lot of what was going on. Night after night, day after day was a struggle to stay composed, and to keep faith. My very quick naps beside my boy were disturbed with the fear of losing him at any moment. I'd whisper to him over and over again how much I loved him and remind him that I'd never leave him. Not long after the nurses around started to encourage me to go home and have a good sleep. They couldn't understand that a parent cannot sleep when their child is on the verge of dying. I didn't leave; I would not leave

Matthew's side. Instead, I had to have my wits about me, to speak up, to ask questions about everything that was being done to him, and then to question the answers. I needed to know everything. I felt then, and I do now, that every parent has that right, to question if they feel they need to understand better what is being done, what is treating what. Therefore, to better understand what is happening and how can a parent be of a healing benefit, both physically, mentally and/or spiritually. Of course, within a few days nurses started to get annoyed with me and tried to keep me outside the ICU and outside of his room, which didn't really work as I had promised my boy, I'd never leave him, and I wholeheartedly meant it.

Two weeks after the first surgery, the doctors performed the second surgery, which lasted 10 hours. Skin was taken from his legs, then applied to his arms and hands. The surgery was supposed to take six hours, but the doctors had to give him a lot of blood transfusions. Waiting and waiting, pacing back and forth, it was wearing out my heart. And on top of that, the nurses wouldn't let me in! I was so filled with anxiety, my heart pounding, and my fears were completely out of control. Not being able to go into the ICU and not being given any answers. My agonizing heart paced through the hallways of despair and my soul started screaming for help. "Help me God!" these words were a plea from a mother that was confined to the fear of hearing the words "your son didn't make it." After what felt like forever, I decided that I was going in no matter what, and nobody could stop me. As I approached the entrance door, through the window I could see a stretcher being pulled into his room. I pushed the door! I was going in! In the same second a nurse walked towards me saying I wasn't allowed.

"Well," I firmly said, "I'm not leaving."

To which she replied, "okay but I need you to just sit down."

"Agreed," I said stoically.

The Challenging Sea of an Awoken Heart

I quickly noticed that a nurse I had never seen before was looking after my son. It's painful to watch your child skinned and stapled, his living flesh struggling to live. While the nurse was connecting and plugging in all of his IV's, his body was literally jumping from the bed shaking with convulsions. Oh, my Jesus! I could literally sense the pain and the shocks in his body! I couldn't keep watching that and asked the nurse to help him. She made the remark that he wasn't having a lot of fun, but in such a manner that I felt enraged for her lack of compassion. I walked away without saying anything further. I marched straight to the nurse station. I pleaded to speak with a doctor immediately. A man who wasn't visible at first rolled his chair out from the back and said that he was a doctor. I asked him to please help my son's body rest. Without a word he got up and walked with me to Matthew's corner of the ICU. There he asked the nurse for something, which she passed to him. It was a syringe, then the doctor administered the sedative to Matthew's IV. Within less than a minute, Matthew's badly hurting body finally started to find peace and the convulsions stopped. I felt incredibly upset, extremely disappointed. In all seriousness, I was a mess of emotions and was feeling very angry. I went back to nurse's station and didn't ask, but demanded that the nurse with my son to be removed. Was I rude? I guess anyone can think what they will, however, I strongly believe that quality care is an obligation of professionals and of everyone who provides it. I think that if I wasn't there, how long would that nurse watch my son 'not having a lot of fun' without helping him or asking for help. My determination strengthened to not ever leave my son alone. I trusted very few people but was definitely very grateful for everyone who's care and love was constant, and the amazing doctors and surgeons that were working so hard to save his life.

The Challenging Sea of an Awoken Heart

Every second or third day I'd run home to shower and change into clean clothes, leaving someone I trusted with Matthew. It's true when I say I had become a target to those who didn't understand my pain, but for those who did understand my heart, they became very kind to me.

WHILE CRYING, NOT KNOWING WHERE TO GO

AND NO ONE CAN HELP YOU,

YOU MUSTN'T GIVE UP, FOR IF YOU DO

ALL THAT YOU LOVE, WILL GIVE UP TOO

(Excerpt from poem "The Hallways of Sadness" in Letters to God – my first book)

The Challenging Sea of an Awoken Heart

One morning, as I returned to the waiting room, I couldn't help but notice that Sandy wasn't there. I went to see if she was with her child, but I was surprised to see that she wasn't there either. I went out into the hallway where I had found her before, she was there, sobbing uncontrollably. As I approached her, she ran from me, and I understood that she needed to be alone.

After about an hour, I decided to walk into the hospital garden, thinking I might find her at the water fountain. She used to cry close to the water, calling it her supply of strength. Indeed, she was there, and I sat with her while she cried. After a while she told me that the medical system wanted to remove her son's life support, as it cost too much money to the system to keep him alive. The news was devastating. I could not believe it! We both cried together at that water fountain. A part of me was that part of her, that part where my heart felt as if it was gasping for air. I told her that whatever she decided to do I'd be by her side every step of the way. After a painful conversation she decided to opt for a petition to fight a system that many times denied the right of living. I don't how she did it, but I too signed the petition, and she won.

Days and nights passed slowly as I sat by my boy's hospital bed and spoke to him softly and reassuringly. I played his music, his CDs, over and over again. Watching some response was like seeing a spark of light in a long dark tunnel.

Outside the world was a different reality. My little business that my two sisters and friends were looking after was, at that point, very hard on them. They too were extremely concerned and fearful for the life of their nephew. They were working their own jobs, dealing with their lives and families, coping with the emotional and long days of work, and it took a beating on them, physical, mentally and spiritually. I will never forget as they tried so hard to help me save my little home, pay my bills, and provide me with some change to eat a little bit at the hospital. Girls, you both have helped me so much and during this most troublesome time of my life, you kept me safe inside your hearts, loving me and giving me strength to go on, making sure that I would not lose my roof and keeping my house safe for me and my little family. You both know who you are and your names are not needed. Words can never express my gratitude for all you've done. If I live to be 100 years old, I'd still not have enough time to thank you. From the deepest part of my heart, I thank you all for everything.

The learning continued from one lesson to another as they certainly arrived with abundance, and I will not go into all the details. But I will say that humanity is headed the wrong way.

Back in the hospital, my reality went from living my fears and pain to fully witnessing it in other people. One evening, a woman arrived at the ICU and from the looks of her she was hurting very much. She had puffed red eyes which were showing signs of a lot of crying and great suffering. She walked in to the little waiting room and looked like she was feeling lost, slowly scanning for a seat, she avoided eye contact. I understood her heart was needing the privacy. Unfortunately, there was only one room for all of us. Some days it was full and some days not so much, but at the end of the day that was our little home and the place where we united during suffering. Oddly enough it was also where we became each other's strength. After some time, she broke the silence by asking me why was I there? From there on she spoke of her reason to be there. Her youngest brother drowned in the family home pool. His heart was still beating, but there was no brain activity. She said, through loud sobs, that she had been a nurse for some time, but that she had no idea what people really experienced in the ICU waiting room. She could never imagine that people could hurt so much.

The truth is, I knew her pain, and there was so much I could've said but I didn't. I gave her a hug and asked her to trust God. A part of me needed that faith, needed to trust. A different part of me had become so separated from Him and didn't really believe that I was worth it of Him, but perhaps she was. I had left God, abandoned Him, as he had not answered my many prayers years before. What I had forgotten is that my prayers had been answered at my very first breath of life.

At this time Matthew's third surgery had been scheduled. The skin on his stomach had grown back enough for the third skin grafts surgery. The doctors were almost done with the skin grafts, but still not a single surgeon could tell me confidently that he would live. The reply to my same question was, we don't know but we are trying our best. The surgery went well and like all the other days and nights I spent it beside his bed. At times crying silently and other times talking to him and begging him to come back to me. Many other times, I just sat there feeling numb, wondering and afraid of the unknown, the next second, and the unpredictable future.

It was the fourth night after the third surgery, around 3AM. He was resting peacefully and I decided to go to the waiting room, which was probably quiet at this time. It was empty. I sat down and felt somewhat grateful for being alone. But something on the long coffee table caught my attention. I had not seen it there in almost 7 weeks of the ICU being my home. A bible was there by itself. Where before there were magazines, now there was only the bible, and my eyes couldn't move away from it. I started to cry. I didn't know what to do. I was confused and scared. Was it there to haunt me? I felt shame and guilt, many different emotions were invading my heart and I didn't know if I was worthy enough to touch it. In truth, I didn't know if judgment was coming for me.

Perhaps an Angel had stopped by for a special delivery. For a special message of some kind. Maybe God still loved me and it was his way of saying, you asked for me, so here I am. About a good 30 minutes passed, and I struggled to decide if I should pick it up or not. At last, I decided to pick it up. Emotionally, I held it close to my heart, while abundant tears ran their course down my face. I hugged it like it was my life; the food for my strength and my soul. It was my everything. Reluctantly, I wondered if I should speak to Him like I used to. It had been so long. I felt such shame for having turned away from Him, not having believed. After a while I found the courage to talk to God. Oh yes, I poured my heart into him. I told him how alone I was feeling, the reasons why I had walked away hoping he would understand. I kept talking, I kept hugging the holy book for I knew that was everything I had. No one else could help ease my pain and my fears. I understood God's loving silent language as he spoke. He said: "My child, you have never left me, you have only left yourself." How could that be? I could not understand. But that did not matter very much at the moment. What was more urgent was my heart, it was in agony. A question was burning inside. Pulling the bible away from my chest, holding it in my shaking hands and staring at it, I asked God, please save my son. Please bring him back to me. Please send me a message that he is going to live.

I randomly opened the bible. I was afraid to see what the message would be, and wiping my tears away so that I could read, my eyes went to a passage close to the middle of one of the pages. I didn't know why, after reading the passage the first, and then the second time, the tears started again, completely out of my control.

It was written:

When you need a miracle, ask God, in the name of your son Jesus Christ to grant you the miracle you're seeking.

Immediately, I knew that God was giving me permission to plea for his life, to ask for the miracle to save my son. As I sat there, I knew the Lord was speaking and in some way that my faith was restored. Filled with an infinite gratitude and remaining with the knowledge of the unknown future, I knew I wasn't alone. I knew my son wasn't alone. In that moment, in the ICU waiting room, the bible and I were everything we had, and for me was so much more than what I had had in a very, very long time. It was everything.

TO BELIEVE IS A MUST, GOD LOVES WHEN WE TRUST

Although no master surgeon or high skilled professional doctor could tell me that Matthew was going to live, I was now filled with hope and faith. Matthew remained on life-assisted support for a while still, but the skin grafts were starting to look good. It had now been close to 2 months in the ICU.

Matthew was moved from Children's Hospital to Vancouver General Hospital's burn unit. There they had a support program and specialists to aid in the recovery of burn patients. Slowly, they begin to decrease the morphine and sedation, it was a slow process. Feeding tubes, breathing tubes, those as well gradually started to be removed, and the day arrived when he opened his beautiful eyes and looked at me for the first time in two months. It was a moment that I had feared would not happen. I was living the most vital moment a mother could live. I didn't cry, I didn't want him to see me cry, but I could cry of gratitude. A gratitude I still feel to this day, and I will be grateful till the day my name gets called to go home.

His eyes were filled with confusion and with questions that he couldn't ask since he couldn't speak. I saw fear, his fear, his tears, and with every attempt to speak he couldn't due to the long time that he was intubated. He had woken up from a two- month sleep and only he could remember the final terrifying and painful moments before he was sedated.

After some time, school friends came to visit. I could see the spark of life reigniting in him, and I knew they had so much to catch up on as soon as he was able to speak and feel a little stronger.

The day came when he was to start trying to walk a little bit. A nurse would come and wrap his legs in compression gauze. He needed this support due to the weakness at the parts of his body where the skin had been removed for the grafts. He was so very weak and very thin. Walking again was of great effort and very difficult for him. He still had many open wounds on his back and his head. I almost forgot to mention that his hair had grown back; his eyebrows and his eyelashes as well were back decorating his beautiful big eyes. I knew he was trying so hard, but with every step and every movement pain would strike and sometimes he would refuse to try again.

My son, you are my idol. I honestly don't know anyone like you, no one who has experienced and lived through so much, and regardless of the times you thought of giving up, you still kept going. My soldier of love, of humbleness and of courage, I couldn't be more grateful for the beautiful human being that God gifted me for a son.

One morning I asked him if he would like to go outside. I knew the outside world he was living in now was different than the one he used to know, but I believed that a little bit of fresh air would be good. Summer was on its way out. He was awake, and I remembered so well the song that I played every night by his bed side: Wake me up when the summer ends. The summer was ending and he was awake. And I was in such deep gratitude. Or emotions that gratitude could never express the depth of itself.

A wheelchair was provided, which I pushed down the hallway and out to the hospital garden. There I found a space with some shade, close to the flowers and also to the busy world that he hadn't seen for two months. The sun tried to caress his face through the dried summer leaves, welcoming him back to life. We didn't talk. My heart was hurting deeply, for I knew he was hurting. I didn't know what to say, especially as I watched a deep sadness invading his face. He didn't move a muscle, not a word and no tears. He just looked lost. Behind the wheelchair, trying to hold my tears from flowing, I made an eternal promise in my heart. My precious son I will never leave you.

Progress was slow but steady. Every day he grew stronger just a tiny bit more than the day before. Our lives have changed forever, no doubt about that. We couldn't change the past, but we could create the future. Soon the day came to go home, and as much I knew the many miles we still had to put in, I was indeed indebted for this miracle. Yes, it was a miracle that I could finally take my son home. I promised myself that every day would start with gratitude and with one step at a time.

Still the open wounds on his back and his head were painful. Bathing was challenging and resistance was fully present. I needed all of my strength to not breakdown. No, breaking down was not an option available to me, at least not as long as he needed my assistance. We were in this together and I wouldn't breakdown. I needed him back playing his drums and filling the house with his music. Most of all I needed him back to life, back to feeling good and happy.

With every single day there was a little bit of improvement. Matthew started getting a little stronger, but as more time passed, I could also see some of the damage would never fully heal. There was so much physical damage, and we still had mental and spiritual healing to work on as well.

Losing months of school year put him behind quite a bit. Eventually he caught up with a lot of extra work and extra help from his school, including night school. But mostly it was him, his amazing personality, his strong will and strong soul helped him through, what I believe, is the hardest ship a human being can ever board and experience during a lifetime. From the moment of the tragedy to these present moments, that were filled with difficulties and with challenges, Matthew's persistence was my light and my strength. I knew he was going to do it. He was going to climb that mountain and then stand up there on the top of the mountain holding the flag of victory. God is good, oh so good.

To this very day, my boy still is the most courageous spirit I have ever known. He is my great friend and I'm blessed to be his mother. I'd like to state here as well my thankfulness for the Surrey Department of Firefighters who cared for and supported us in different ways. I wish that God continues to bless them and keep them and their loved ones safe at all times. I honestly don't know anyone else who deserves as much respect as they do.

The Challenging Sea of an Awoken Heart

I had so much healing to do. So much had happened in the last few months and I knew that a different version of Maria had resurrected. A Maria that no longer doubted God and a Maria that needed to forgive. I had so much forgiving to do, including forgiving myself, but mostly the people who almost had killed my son, everyone involved. While trying to find ways to start the forgiveness process, a sad reality knocked on my door. It was extremely disappointing and hurtful to realize that, after becoming victims of a crime, we were in many ways becoming victims of our systems. I cried and cried, and couldn't believe what my eyes were reading over and over again. I'll just leave this subject here because systems have spies being overpaid to protect their poor heartless work. Out of that came an even more sad realization that many other parents had gone through the same or similar circumstances without the right of being heard and being served with what was just. Unfortunately, some systems after tragedy will strip out our dignity and shred our souls, and still claim it as the laws of justice, which do not have anything to do with any kind of quality care for humanity or our Canadian born children.

It's hard to accommodate this painful awareness that we are living under controlling and fearful mentalities, and certainly impossible to digest the ingredients which are being served to most of us. But it's called law, it's called healthy living, it's called religions and societies. It makes me feel sick. Still, I couldn't allow anything or anyone to blur the light I could now see, the love I could now feel, and the gratitude that was my every heartbeat. The God I knew was real, and I really wanted to try to help humanity find Him, even if only a glimpse of Him.

The Challenging Sea of an Awoken Heart

We are love, not hate

We are love, not dictators

We are eternal life, not time

We are the light, not the tunnel

We are each others way

Let's be each other's light.

The Challenging Sea of an Awoken Heart

Chapter 11

We Are Born From Pure Love, Why Can't We All Live To Love

Little by little I aimed to fulfill what I had in my heart, to share love, to help people understand that they too were love. But believe me that humans do put up a lot of resistance when it comes to opening to something larger and greater than what they believe they are. They refuse welcoming a better version of themselves. Resistance has and still is one of human's worst enemy, especially resistance to growth and embracing the new.

Ok, now we go back a bit to the healing process, which wasn't easy. I was a mess. My sleep was completely messed up. It was filled with anxieties and waking up to panic attacks was a regular phenomenon. I would find myself shaking with cold sweats, my heart pounding. I'd run and check on my son, making sure he was still breathing, making sure he was alive. I was traumatized and the fears of the last several months were haunting me during all hours of my days and my nights. I then would go into periods of crying, of praying and of asking for divine assistance, of asking for divine intervention. I prayed and prayed, and I still do. I know I also have been heard and I have no doubt that God is good and He loves everyone just as much as He loves me.

I TRULY WISH THAT ALL OF HUMANITY GETS TO KNOW HIS LOVE, FOR HIS LOVE IS LOVE

As I mentioned earlier in the book, I had an experience in which I met a lady with silver hair. One day, on the way to work with my sister, we decided to stop at the mall to take a look at the book store, as we loved to read metaphysical books. This was something we did quite often as we loved to see if there were any exciting new arrivals.

We happily arrived and started looking around. My sister quickly got lost in between the stands and shelves while I was slowly moving forward to make sure I wouldn't miss out on anything that would catch my eye. At the beginning of one of the isles there was a sign saying New Arrivals. I walked towards the display of new arrivals and the very first book my eyes landed on was called "Eyes of an Angel." On the cover there was also a picture of a woman that wasn't clearly visible, so I walked closer and looked at the picture. I felt mesmerized as I realized that it was same woman I had seen before. She was an angel. No, I was not mistaken! I could still feel the beautiful energy of love, something I've never forgotten. I felt so grateful and immediately purchased the book. I feel I should mention that the name of the author is Paulo Elder, and he was a resident of North Vancouver. The book was based on true events of his life.

In that moment, I had no idea I was about to start experiencing some of the most unforgettable moments of my life. I was just incredibly excited and looked forward to reading this new book. It felt like I had just won the lottery. Or even better than that, I believe that money cannot purchase this kind of experience. The most fascinating experiences of a lifetime. Looking back, it was a heavenly lottery.

As soon we were finished work, I got home, spend some time with the kids and then retreated to my room, which was my sacred space and my sanctuary. I lit a candle and made myself comfortable. I started reading the book and bit by bit my thirst for more was growing. I eagerly read each page to get to the next, and then the next chapter. The first couple of nights were fascinating and I'd have a hard time waiting for the following night with the excitement of what was going to happen next. Finally, it happened, the third night of starting this book, that was when my spiritual life was enlightened in such divine ways that my life wouldn't ever be the same again.

I got comfortable in my bed, just like the previous nights, and picked up my book. I started where I had left off the night before. I was reading for about twenty minutes, and as I was holding the book something started to happen that felt very weird. At first, I didn't pay much attention to it, but it was consistent. I felt that my fingers were stuck to the book, but in my mind, there was no way I was going to stop reading. I thought: "Whatever! Get me stuck anywhere but don't take my book away!" I was loving it too much and didn't feel like interrupting it for anything. But the vibrational sensation was just getting out of control and at that point I was certain that my fingers were definitely glued to the book. I was not happy at all! I wasn't scared, but I decided to check it out by gently moving my fingers one by one, and to my great relief I found they were able to move freely. Happily, I went straight back to reading. The peace, however, didn't last long. I soon felt as if something was happening in my room. I lifted my eyes and saw an angel, a figure of light, rising from the floor. The being of light was becoming bigger and brighter. The entire wall in front of me was soon blocked by this heavenly being, an angelic shape of light. An enormous vibration took complete control of my body as I felt I was in a vortex of pure energy.

I WAS, I AM. WE ARE PURE LOVING ENERGY IN PURE WHITE LIGHT

The Challenging Sea of an Awoken Heart

Now I started to feel frightened. My very first thought was to jump out of bed, run out of my room, and even out of the house, but I couldn't move as quickly as something unexplainable was starting to unfold. As I moved my hands to pull the covers off me, suddenly something very wonderful and magical happened. It felt like a warm and comforting blanket was being ever so gently and lovingly placed over me. It started with my feet, and gradually covering every part of my body until I was completely embraced, cozy, and tucked in, in this cocoon of eternal Love. It was an overwhelming sensation of warmth, pure love and divine peace that took over my whole existence in that moment. My fears were gone and I was feeling loved and cared for like I've never felt before. I realized this kind of love was pure perfection, there was no past, no future, only this moment. The perfect eternal moment. No suffering, no pain, no fears, just that pure safe and peaceful Love.

I knew I would never ever be or feel alone again. As I laid there in my bed with this feeling of deep gratitude, I saw this very large beautiful being of Love and Light slowly begin to break down into smaller Angels of Light, filling up my room with divine white being with wings. Was I in Heaven? Nope, just in my bed in my room, but it sure felt like the perfect heaven to live in forever.

After some time, they all slowly started to fade away. I couldn't move, and I didn't want to move. I just stayed still enjoying these feelings. Shortly after my eyes saw another appearance. It was a pen. It was a pen of light, a long pen of light, and it slowly moved right above my eyes. It gently drew a beautiful heart of white light. And just as the previous event, it gently faded away. After some time, I still was speechless and entranced by loving emotions I didn't know I had. I didn't want that feeling to end; I didn't want to get back to my normal life. I didn't want to go back to experience again and again the experience of pain or the low emotions that we humans are subjected to feel. After these divine encounters I knew that Love, the love that humans speak of, is so different from the Divine Love that we truly are. I needed this Love to never ever leave me. Honestly, I would have been more than happy to stay there for the rest of my life.

The Challenging Sea of an Awoken Heart

Thank you, Heaven! Thank you, God and his assistants! Inside my heart I thank them over and over again with the promise to celebrate them and to share with others that divine Love that in truth is available to us all. Right there, in that moment, I started practicing forgiveness. I emerged from this divine encounter a changed person. So much had happened in such a short time and I was filled with humbleness, and with humility. Deep down in my heart I knew that what I had experienced was in fact the truth of our divine souls, our eternal lives. We are that Love and that Light. I then realized how trapped we humans are. It's deeply painful to know this. We are trapped in everything that is so small, that blocks us from learning the completion and richness of opportunities we are gifted with. To remember this True Love while living Love on Earth.

At the end of the day, I fully understood. We really are only each other's reflection; each other's fears, each other's strengths, and each other's weaknesses. We are each other's darkness, and each other's light. I promised myself to do the best I possibly could at releasing and letting go everything that was not my light, and that didn't bring light to my Light and to my life.

While staring at my empty room and replaying the angel apparition in my mind, I felt as if I had lived pieces of my past lives. Those lives I've lived before but not on Earth; lives I lived in higher dimensions and higher frequencies. That pure Love I felt enlightened by was to a certain degree familiar, bringing to life dormant memories from ancient times, and a re-awakened faith I knew existed before.

I decided to give myself a couple of weeks break before returning to reading my book. I honestly had so much to think about and to learn from the angelic encounter, and I didn't want anything new to delay my learning process from this experience that I just had.

That was my wish, not to be interrupted with anything else, but it didn't last long because every night that I returned to my room I was filled with a very high energy frequency, and sometimes I didn't like it because I couldn't control it. I did the only thing I could think of, I would pray and do grounding meditations until I'd finally fall asleep.

One night, in the early morning hours, when I suddenly was wide awake but my room was still dark. Or so I thought. I tried to look for the outside lights from my bedroom window, as I sometimes did, but for some reason I was confused why I couldn't see the window. Adjusting to the dark, and trying to scan all around my room, I realized I could see entities slowly moving around my bed. It's like they were there, kind of waiting for me to wake up, or something like that. I thought, did you guys get the wrong address? I was not impressed or ready for those kinds of visitors. Are you kidding? Couldn't you find any better entertainment? To put it differently, I was paralyzed by fear. So, in my heart I started to pray for them to go away as I pulled the covers over my head. I don't know for how long I was praying; all I know is that the next time I checked they were all gone. I felt so relieved. I could then see the window and the walls and the outside lights. I was sure I didn't want to see them again.

After that, I understood that I could see them. I could see ghosts, entities, even animals that had passed. I was open but very vulnerable to their apparitions, but I needed to learn how to create boundaries, and to protect myself. And they needed to understand that I wasn't okay with the invasion of privacy in any way.

So how do I create a boundary with a ghost? It was kind of like, 'you guys stay in your world and I'll stay in my world. Let's not invade each other's space or privacy without an invite, okay?!'

I started doing meditations to help me ground more and protect myself, and somehow those were of comfort, but they didn't work the way I expected.

I faithfully continued praying for protection and peace, it only lasted for couple of nights, but better than nothing. A little progress is better than no progress at all.

The Challenging Sea of an Awoken Heart

On the next day, a Saturday, at around 6AM, I got up to go to the bathroom. As I returned to my room, leaving the ensuite bathroom door open like I always did, I stepped into bed, and started to pull the bed covers over me. Within an instant the craziest wind along with stormy whistling, started to blow from the direction of the bathroom, and started to blow the covers away from me. For one second, I thought: what crazy stuff is this? This cannot be happening to me! With both my hands I pulled the covers with all my strength to cover myself, but the harder I tried the stronger the wind would blow. Tired of the insanity, I screamed out: "what is happening?" I started to yell at the top of my lungs, a mouth full of honestly not nice words. I was so enraged; I was really mad. Well, that worked because the truth is the calm came, the howling storm and everything stopped. When I think of it, boy, was I glad there was no lightening. But the rainbow never came either! Silence took over and I felt pretty freaking grateful. What the heck had just happened? I asked myself, who the heck was that, that tried to scare the life out of me? I didn't know, but I was certain that we would never be friends. I like to be warmth, so to take my blankets is never a good idea!

My next step, I thought, I would like to find someone that could do a spiritual reading for me. I needed to find out what it was that these spirits wanted with me. I started to ask around if anyone knew someone providing psychic services. Before too long I found a lady that did Angel card readings, and happily I made an appointment to see her a couple of days later. The day arrived and I was eager for my session. I was filled with hope that the lady could also tell me about how to keep the entities away in my day-to-day life. When I arrived, the woman invited me in and gestured to sit by a small table. On the table were a white candle, burning silently, and a beautiful tower-point of rose quartz crystal. The energy was of love and peace, but for some reason I was feeling anxious and nervous. The reading started off well and what she was telling me was mostly accurate. She had messages from my Angels. Yes, my angels! I thought, I like that, and the fears started to vanish. I actually started to feel at peace, but that too didn't last very long. At that point the woman said to me that I would be talking to dead people. I was utterly shocked; I was petrified and almost fell of my chair. Standing up and terminating the services, I said: "No, I don't think so! I don't want anything to do with them." I got up and paid for the reading and left. I wanted to run away, run fast and not look back!

Walking away from my new reality. That's what I was doing, and I felt vulnerable and so very scared. I kept praying and meditating. Some nights were better than others; some peaceful and some with unpleasant events. I decided to meditate before going into my room to sleep, so getting into bed and pulling the bed covers over me, I'd lay down with a prayer inside my heart. That felt right for a while. Until about a week later, I woke up, outside of my body. My soul was fully awake and active in a strange place that I had never seen before. I could see that my body was sleeping, kind of like being in two places at once, but this other place felt like a lower dimension, and its density was of a very low vibration. There were voices that I couldn't understand, but the feeling was of a deep sense of sadness and pain. A pain that was not my pain. I could only see silhouettes, strangely and slowly moving like lost entities. A strange fog surrounded them and was also around me, and it seemed to be getting thicker and colder. I was starting to feel I couldn't breathe, the cold moisture gripped my lungs, and my visibility throughout the foggy dimension was very heavy and blurry.

What was this place? This question was screaming in my soul, when suddenly I just knew - it was purgatory. This was the place where souls were stuck, unable to move on towards the Light. These souls were souls that had passed away from tragic passings, tragic events, others from poor ways of living life on earth while they lived, from being careless towards their fellow humans, from greed and from criminal actions, from addictions, and from suicide. These souls were in truth free to move on but they couldn't because of the pain they had inflicted on others had become their pain, their guilty conscience was their penalty, their penance and their suffering was real. I fell to my knees as I felt their suffering and asked God to help them find the Light and find the peace they so needed to find and keep. Most of all, to help them forgive themselves as I know in my heart that God always forgives us all. Especially when we ask God for forgiveness.

In that moment, I remembered my mother's words to me when I was a young girl; the many times she'd remind me of how important it was to pray for all souls who were in purgatory. She was right. And I also ask you readers to please take a minute to pray for them because I know that that dimension is real, those souls were real. For I've seen them, I have been there, and that experience was as real as every breath that keeps me alive. Life in the afterlife is not always a peaceful life. In fact, during that experience I understood that it is very much like life on earth, but with a different vibration, a different energy frequency. Here on earth the suffering is held in a physical form, and in the afterlife, it is held in a memory imprint. However, when souls move on freely into higher dimensions of love and light, they will many times show themselves in the form very much like they were before passing from the physical to spiritual realms, or they'll be surrounded by a beautiful translucent white light. Their vibrations are of pure love and they can communicate with us humans in a frequency of peaceful energy, that leaves us feeling filled with a sense of endless love. I will come back to this subject a little later as I have so much to share with you all.

IF PEOPLE COULD SEE THEIR SOULS IN THE MIRROR, INSTEAD OF THEIR FACES, THEY WOULD BE A LOT KINDER

The Challenging Sea of an Awoken Heart

During these challenging times of a powerful awakening, in which Spirit didn't ask me for permission to take over my life, to disturb my sleep, to invade my space and my privacy. I really tried to understand what was going on and my search was still on to find someone who could help me with learning its knowledge, and also to help me lower my chakras vibrations because most of the time I felt as if I was plugged into electricity. Sure, you can laugh, right now I too do laugh at it, but believe me when I say that, there was no fun when it was happening, and I was being hunted down like there was no tomorrow.

Well, sometime later a friend of mine, who I had not spoken with for a while, told me of a lady who was a very good psychic in Las Vegas and suggested I give her a call. Thanking her I took the number as if it was a miracle pill and the next day, I gave the miracle worker a call.

"Hello," the other end of the line was answered by a gentle voice. Somehow it felt as she wasn't feeling well or going through some issues of her own. I was a little uncertain whether to go ahead, but my desire for help was stronger and desperately needed. Whatever it was, she was sweet and pleasant and was very attentive to what I thought were real problems in my life. She stayed quiet while I poured out my heart and soul, then when I had finished, she softly said to me, "Maria, don't you worry, you are just like me, but you don't know how to control the gifts God in Heaven gifted you with."

She asked if she could take a minute to say a prayer, and that I would feel better.

"Okay" I said and hung on the line in silence for her return.

She came back shortly after and said that my vibration should be lowering very shortly. In fact, it was basically immediately. My legs and my feet didn't feel like electrical posts or antennas, my head wasn't feeling like a balloon up in the atmosphere anymore. I could feel almost normal and grounded and in charge of my mind and thoughts. She really was a miracle worker that helped me so much! She also suggested some books for me to read that would help me educate myself along my spiritual path.

Edgar Cayce (born 1877 and passed 1945), known as the sleeping prophet, this amazing man that had walked the earth long before I was borne. His books and his spiritual knowledge, his wisdom, his love was my very first best friend along the path I am on now. Through reading his books, he taught me so much about my spiritual journey and my spiritual gifts. Thank you, Edgar Cayce. I believe you are still helping and healing along your multidimensional journey.

So, with that I decided to read all I could find on Edgar Cayce. I started to practice the exercises in his books, to practice grounding and protection. I also learned that I am the boss of myself and no spirit was really allowed to come to me without being invited. With that, I faithfully took charge of my spiritual destiny; becoming of service between worlds, between spirits and humans, between healing and suffering, between hate and love, between fear and faith, between darkness and light, between sickness and health and definitely between life and death.

When in control and comfortable enough with my gifts, I started to invite Spirit into my life. What previously had been a disturbing quiet time, started to become a sacred time, a time of connecting to a higher power, I call it God. For he is God and God is real. Also, angels would show up in so many different beautiful ways. Those times with the Divine I knew I was protected and safe. I knew regardless of what lay ahead, I wouldn't be alone. I saw spirits of people who had passed away when I was a young girl. Some were faded memories or perhaps those who I so devotedly visited prior to their funeral, or those I looked at, while they looked like in deep sleep, and placed a kiss on their cheek before leaving their side. I was definitely a very different kid and the idea of death never really fitted in my heart and my soul. I'd get messages for people from their deceased loved ones and gave them a call, some appreciated it and some, well not so much. That was okay, for my job was to do my job and not theirs.

There has always been and there will always be the believers and the non-believers. Either way, we are all students in different grades and different class rooms. This was my new life, and with it the many adventures that were about to add to my life on earth as a spiritual activist, a spiritual leader of love working for the good of all.

It was the beginning of the beginning, as I now know there's no ending. Don't get me wrong for I am human like you and as you now know I too had faced challenges and hardships of many different kinds. I still do but have learned to deal with everything in a much different way and manner.

With this deeper understanding of my gifts and how to live with them in a safe way, I knew that I could not hide from the call. And definitely never from being chosen to walk the path, the path of healing on Earth. I made the decision to start doing spiritual sessions for people who were looking for divine guidance, or that were looking to connect with passed on loved ones. One morning as I had just opened the door to the public, and this gentleman walked in. He looked unsure or somehow a little nervous. I wished him a good morning and asked if I could be of help. He replied: "yes, but I don't really believe in this kind of thing."

I told him that I understood, which I truly did, and invited him to try it anyway. I added that he could stop at any moment if that was his wish. He agreed and before too long he had tears rolling down his cheeks. When the session came to an end, he was deeply grateful that it had given him so much clarity on how to proceed about his life, and all that he had to do accordingly to his own and to his family's highest good.

"How do you know these things?" he asked.

"I don't, but God does, I only deliver the message and all the credits go to God that oversees us at all times."

I believe that that morning his life had changed, that he wouldn't linger in the dark anymore because he knew that only God could know all that he knew.

My journey was beautiful, and the bliss of pure love that guided my heart and my soul to trust God, trust the guidance, trust the call that was leading my way of living. I have not chosen this path. I was chosen, and I promised that I would follow Him and would always try my best to never disappoint my holy leader.

CAN YOU PROVE THAT GOD IS REAL? WELL, CAN YOU PROVE THAT HE ISN'T?

I also was tested by the skeptics at different times and not in a very nice way. People are scared of what they cannot understand, and the saddest of it all is that they don't want to understand. They prefer to judge and to speak poorly of a knowledge they refuse to learn anything about. That's alright by me, but it's never okay to be offensive. One time, I was asked to prove that God is real. I replied also with a question, can you prove that he is not? No answer! The individual walked away and I never heard from that person again.

My journey was so filled with different things every day. The different experiences and different people that brought the opportunities to practice perfection quite often. I felt it, that it was perfect. Not having boring moments kept me learning all the time. And as the word spread, I started to get busier with people needing help in many different ways. I clearly remember this one young woman that came in for a spiritual reading, and as the session went on, bringing to her attention the messages to pay attention to her heart. The truth is, it became a very annoying experience for us both because the message was just screaming at me, in which I really had to stress this fact to her a number of times. 'Please be aware of your heart or any symptoms that may not feel right.' But she refuted what I said every time. She also got annoyed and replied that she had a very healthy heart and that the message did not resonate with her. The session came to an end and she left somewhat irritated.

I don't really recall the exact time frame, but it was a good six months later, when a young woman walked into my metaphysical space, walked up straight to me asking if I remembered her, which of course I didn't. But she said that I had done a session for her and warned her about her heart.

"Oh yes," I replied, "I remember that."

She went on to tell me that not long after our session, while in middle of some chores at home, she suddenly started to experience chest pain. She continued with her tale and had remembered the message from our session. She immediately called the 911 emergency line. When the paramedics arrived, she had collapsed and had suffered a massive heart attack. She was taken to the hospital and had open heart surgery. In that moment, she opened the top two buttons on her blouse, showing me the large scar on her chest. She was in tears, as she added that she had died during surgery for a couple of minutes. While being in this state, she saw the most beautiful white light and she didn't want to come back because it was so perfect and free of pain. She also watched the surgeons and nurses trying to resuscitate her. She hugged me and thanked me for guiding her. She said that if it wasn't for the message, she probably wouldn't have called 911 right away.

Hugging her back I said: "It wasn't me that saved you, it was God. His Love for you saved you!"

Right there in that moment of truth and eternal Love, was my God letting me know that every step I took towards helping humanity, He would take two steps towards helping me.

Don't ever regret being a good person,

or doing good to others.

What you do to others will be done to you.

What you give will be given to you.

Remember to be generous.

The Challenging Sea of an Awoken Heart

Chapter 12

If We All Pray For Someone, We All Have Someone Praying For Us

I started sleeping better, but while asleep I wasn't in control of what was laying ahead. My adventurous soul which was always looking for a new experience.

I had made prayer my priority before laying down to sleep, but fell asleep before my prayer was completed. So that one night I decided I wasn't going to lay down, I was just going to lean back on my pillows and make sure I wasn't going to fall asleep while praying. I made myself comfortable and was pretty happy with making the right choice.

Let the prayers begin! I was completely in it and feeling overcome by a very deep peace, when suddenly I realized I was standing by my bed looking at myself in bed praying. Wow, are you for real? Is that me? It was me indeed! How fascinating, I thought, while looking at myself.

"That is me and I don't even know that I'm seeing me."

I was mesmerized by it all! I realized that somehow, I looked different; I was of pure peace, I was love, and I was just fine with all that I was.

I started to look at the beautiful light blue colour of the walls in my room, and I could swear that they could speak, like they had a heartbeat. I resonated with that divine vibration. I understood that nothing existed outside of me but everything exists through me, and I existed through everything. In truth nothing exists outside of me, or that beautiful living blue, that it's all connected, and that is perfect. No explanation needed, because I understood that life lives through everything and that everything breathes the never-ending breath of eternal life.

Of course, after this beautiful awareness I thought of using my time out-of-my-body to check everything around the room, and perhaps maybe take a trip to Portugal or somewhere else. Haha! I felt like laughing but didn't want to disturb Maria while she was praying. I started to check the room by scanning every wall back to the window, and slowly to the board at the foot of my bed. I didn't want to miss anything, or any detail. Everything was alive, and I was beyond happy and grateful. Well, until that moment, when I saw someone standing at the foot of my bed looking at the Maria that was praying. That individual entity was wearing a long black cape with a black hood, and I couldn't see his face. But I was already sure I didn't like him.

Was he the reaper? What did he want from her? I didn't want to find out because I kept wanting to enjoy my time free from my physical life. And I really didn't have time to die! He was very tall. While I was still thinking of finding my way around without being seen, I was suddenly back in my body. All had come to an end. I wasn't happy. I didn't know, and still don't know, what happened or how it happened, but I didn't have any control over the situation. I still don't know who he was. I'm okay with that now. I promised myself that if there would be a next time, I would go to the Azores Islands for a quick visit.

During the many different experiences and also challenges with Spirit, I also experienced different parts of past lives. It's hard to explain how it happened, as I didn't try to or did anything different, it just happened and still happens.

One of those times I found myself in Egypt as a young woman. I believe I was poor due to the very simple and worn-out garments. I was hugging a little child's coffin and crying. I looked at the coffin; it was very rustic, like a rough piece of wood nailed to another piece of wood, it wasn't polished or nicely finished. It had cracks in between the nailed pieces of wood. I felt invaded by a deep but faraway sadness. I knew that I had lost my baby and that I couldn't let go. I also got the sense that I was all alone. However, I knew that was then, in a past life, and that in this present life, I felt the grief and the emotional pain. Somehow, I knew it resonated with my present life and the fear of losing my children.

I was also shown pieces of another past life, which was in Italy. There I was around seventeen years of age, a beautiful and graceful, red haired and nicely cared for girl. I also knew that being a red-head was the reason I was always kept inside the house. For whatever all the other reasons as well, it was to keep me safe. I had very light, silky, beautiful skin, and I could fully see and feel that I was being raised by a wealthy family. I wasn't ever allowed to leave my home. For some reason, this time, I was out of the house and walking down a little steep hill surrounded by little houses. I was so happy and feeling so free. The little girl who I was holdings hands with, was around eight or nine years of age, and she too was feeling happy. I didn't know how, but I knew she was my sister then, and at the same time I knew she was my mother in this life-time. Suddenly a freezing cold, dead breeze went straight through my bones. I didn't know why, but I started to check around for anything that could be dangerous. On one side of the cul-du-sac, and in between two houses, there was a man hiding and intently looking at me. He had something black over his head and face in a way that the only thing I could see was the open circles that allowed him to see. I felt scared and looked to the other side of the road. I saw someone riding a white horse at high speed. I fully knew that the horse rider was trying to save me. What followed was like anything else unknown and unpredictable. The next thing I knew I was laying on the ground lifeless. I had been murdered, and with no doubt because I was a red head and considered a witch.

Some years later on I came across the knowledge of who the horse rider was. This left me speechless. It is someone that has been in my present life, who was hunted by fear and held a deep belief that having red hair is bad luck. This present moment awareness, gave me full understanding where the fears were coming from. This individual and I had had past lives together.

I strongly feel I must share this with you now. Napoleon, and you probably know who I'm referring to when I use this name. Yes, THE Napoleon! In this past-life experience I just shared, Napoleon and the rider are different individuals but the same soul in different reincarnations. And in that moment, he was part of my life.

It makes me acknowledge the truth of the many times we keep reincarnating into each other's lives in order to heal past lives karma and unfinished business.

In an out-of-body experience that followed, I found myself walking inside a place down a cold and dark hallway. I got the sense that it was a jail. It was underground, and the air was dank and unpleasant. The walls were made of what looked like humid clay. I could see long hallways with tiny little faded lights that illumined only small areas. As I scanned around to see which direction I should go towards, I felt confused as all directions looked the same, and also felt the same. However, I decided to start walking in one direction and see if I could find someone that could direct me to the person I was trying to visit.

Yes, I was there for a visit. It was a prisoner I was looking for, and finally after some time of walking around, I could see the silhouette of a woman. I happily walked towards her. She had a look of surprise on her face to see me there in front of her. I didn't know why, but it didn't matter to me because I was there with a purpose. I told her I was there to see Jack Fraser (fictious name), and this made her very confused. I insisted that I was there to see him, and I knew that he was there.

At this point I will mention that I had a young boy with me, and that he was mine and this man's son.

The woman looked at the two of us with great annoyance as if she wasn't understanding who I was looking for. For some unknown reason the next words flew out of my mouth without my intention, like a lightening flash from memory, I said: "I'm here to see Napoleon."

Immediately, her annoyance left, and she comprehended who I was referring to. Then she indicated for me to follow her as she started walking down one of the long dark corridors. We stopped by a large iron door with a very tiny little iron window. She opened the small barred window and left us there, and walked away without saying anything further.

I called him through the little window a few times before I could see fragile skinny fingers coming through the little iron bars of the window.

My fingers caressed his fingers and I told him that our child was doing well. His murmurs were fainted and weak, and he slowly started to retreat, pulling his fingers away. And that was the end of my another past-life encounter.

This was a just a small peak into my past life with Napoleon. I wonder if I was his wife. I don't know for certain, but I do know that the boy was ours, and I also know that that boy was and is in my life now. I do know that this person, Jack Fraser, was in my present life for 10 years. Just for your knowledge, and to my awareness, I witnessed how Jack Fraser also felt a strong connection to this boy when they met in this life. And how when everyone was together, he couldn't take his eyes off him with so many children in the family, he certainly favoured one that he barely saw.

The question remained; was he ever open to learning beyond numbers? Because numbers are Jack's career. Nope, never, and that was okay. This book, my life, is about my journey, but my journey is completed by every relationship, every person, and every event that I've lived through in this life. I've learned while this man was in my life for these 10 years, that he was not just Napoleon but also the horse rider from a different past life. As I wrote about earlier, the rider tried to save me and lost me because I was killed due to my red hair.

I've witnessed the same fear in Jack's face, when one day, I had coloured my hair from blonde to red. Really just to piss him off because I knew he loved blonds. The outcome was shocking; he looked like he was having a panic attack. He couldn't even move while looking at me with my new red hair. I saw the extreme fear on his face while he whispered over and over again the question: "what have you done?"

It makes me shake my head, and question whether it's just random crazy events or that everything has an explanation. I know from all these past life experiences and insights there are no coincidences. Everything has a reason, this is certain.

A few days later I asked him what was the big deal and the panic mode with the red hair? He sadly replied: "it means bad luck." I can't help wonder, was that his dormant memory from that past life that we had together? I know, for sure it was, but could we ever talk about any of that? No, impossible, because he was brought up in such restricted religious conditions that left him trapped inside the seven-year-old little boy, watching tv in a dark basement by himself while mommy attended church, and who believed that he was condemned by sins. This never allowed him to get to know his Higher Self in any way, or even the possibility that there is life after life and that we keep coming back over and over again in order to heal and in order to evolve as spiritual beings.

The Challenging Sea of an Awoken Heart

Many years have passed and I believe that he is still there in the same frame of mind. But that's no longer my issue. I can't help anyone that doesn't want to help themselves, or that helps me evolve in my spiritual path with a greater and bigger Light.

The story didn't end there. My purpose in Jack's life in this lifetime wasn't finished. I had to be there for him and claim his rights to live during extreme sickness and painful life-threatening illnesses. He was the kind of person that was never open to certain amusements, and certainly against all my beliefs, and against my love for God.

I did a lot of research about Napoleon, and it is astounding that even Jack's facial features, characteristics, similarities, and the extreme phobias about being poisoned, all these were also in his present life. These were part of his demons and realities, or so it seemed. They were pieces of past life traumas and memories.

Napoleon was taken exile to Saint Helena the Costa. It was under British rule in the middle of the Atlantic Ocean, and he was left there on October fifteen in 1815.

Life is a great mystery with no beginning and no ending. Just like the ocean, no one knows where it begins or were it ends. It is impossible to fully understand it all, but that is okay, because as we move along, we eventually start understanding a little more about it. We find the little pieces of the great puzzle that we are, and there will be the time when we magically will understand where each piece of the puzzle belongs and goes to help us understand most of everything we don't understand. Not only that, but also, in time, it all makes perfect sense, there was never a mistake. There was always what we knew then verses what we learned, and then what we come to know.

The most important lessons of life are learned along the way with the many different kinds of people and different personalities and nationalities.

Relationships are the greatest teachers we have during our time on earth, and I certainly believe that one must be great at teaching but also great at learning. Yet it is so very important to want to learn, and sometimes to learn to learn is a must!

The Challenging Sea of an Awoken Heart

What makes you happy,

You do that.

What makes your heart feel excited,

You chose that.

What challenges you,

You chase that.

What you love to wear best,

You wear that.

Life is wild,

let you live the wilderness of your endless soul,

for nothing can substitute experience.

The Challenging Sea of an Awoken Heart

Chapter 13

My Body Of Light

These past lives experiences, and out of body experiences, they kept happening. Not because I tried but they just happened naturally, and I fell so deeply in love with it all. It was so revealing to learn about the past, the infinity of the present, and the never ending of the future, and how it all fit so perfectly into the puzzle piece of my current life.

Apparitions, or Spirit manifested, yes, that happened too and still does. If you ask me about how normal it feels, I'd say it's okay but not as fun as being outside of my body.

When my soul is free of my body, I can do anything, go places, see people. Honestly, this free traveling is pretty awesome and filled with a divine joy and freedom. That is where differences don't exist, everything is a divine and a united love.

It's a kind of divine freedom and intelligence that lives through every single life. Every tree leaf, every seed, every cloud and every drop of water. I feel deeply humbled with all the love and wisdom in which everything was so perfectly programmed and correlated.

In all honesty, it makes me feel emotional thinking about the infinite wisdom, that everything has the intelligence of choosing one thought after the other in order to create or recreate its own self. That accordingly to the divine creator, God, all has been so perfectly programmed and organized to keep on living eternally on both sides of life, and not outside of any life. To keep on giving life to all others lives. We see this clearly in nature itself, nothing is wasted. A tree leaf nurtures its own mother, the tree, in the soils from which it grows. And so on. There is no ending to it.

Speaking of spiritual encounters, I'd like to share that later on after my brother in-law passed away, Lucia's husband, I have seen him in three different occasions. The first one in which he clearly showed me the last seconds of his life, while he was driving his motorcycle. He was petrified by the truck that had missed the stop sign, and driving straight at him.

He was hectically trying to change gears, knowing that time was not in his favour, but with every foot movement on the metal lever, his wet rubber boots would slip off the lever, and he was unable to shift gears. Every attempt was unsuccessful to the moment he was hit. It's tragic, his passing came with extreme injuries.

He precisely stressed the fact that he tried to save himself. He constantly was bringing my attention to his last moments' efforts. Then he saw that I fully understood the message, and it all came to an end and he vanished.

Another time and back in time, I was able to see him when he was dating my sister, Lucia. I wasn't living on the island anymore, but it was very interesting to bring some information back to Lucia. I was on the lower road, and he was with my sister on the higher level of the road. I could see them when I was looking up, and his look indicated that he could see me too when he looked down onto the lower road.

My sister wasn't aware of my presence but was busy in romancing Manuel, and, I could feel he was uncomfortable with my presence. He was conservative and not okay being watched, but I really didn't choose to be there.

They were sitting up on the cliff, high up from the ocean below, overlooking the endless sea. This side of the road was perfect for young romance because it offered a long concrete wall and a beautiful view. I could perfectly see the colour of his shirt and the clothes that he was wearing, which I later shared with her. And she fully confirmed that they had been there, and also confirmed the clothes and colour of the T-shirt.

Life doesn't ever end. Our souls are eternal and can manifest themselves in different places at the same time, because Spirit knows no time. Our bodies of light can be seen in the divine light and the many different dimensions, meaning our souls can see each other. Spirit is eternal love and love never dies.

Similar to these, many other episodes have happened, and I wouldn't want life to be any different as this is perfect. This growth and this divine eternal life on this side of life is beyond belief and precious. My divine guide of love is God. I don't have any doubt that the voice inside my house was God, which still leads me and guides me at all times.

It's always that voice, His voice.

I was driving along Highway 15. It was another busy day rushing from one place to another to honour my commitments, look after my family, and meet my needs. This was around 2008 and like every other day I was always short on time to attend to some stuff that needed attention. It was my minivan, which for a couple of weeks was indicating it needed the brakes fixed, but I kept pushing my luck until the next day.

It wasn't smart, I know, but I was never good at mechanical issues and like I said, I was always short on time.

I was driving the speed limit, around 80 kilometers per hour. My sister was with me, since we worked together, and in the rush to the next job we suddenly heard a loud voice shouting to slow down. My sister and I looked at each other perplexed, and I asked her if she had heard that, which she confirmed that she did, and once more the voice shouted again to slow down. Okay! I got the message! I started to brake, to fully become aware that I didn't have any brakes. A panic sensation tried to take over my senses, but a sudden strange calm and peace came over me, and I started to gently pump the brakes. By doing so I was able to come to a full stop at the intersection without any accidents or tragedies. Luck isn't the correct word; the right word is blessed. God is good! I sure am grateful that he helped me save myself, my sister, and the other people that like me who were also driving and going about their lives.

I will also speak of another time. A time I was working evenings from 5.30PM to about 11 or 11.30PM. That night, during a little break with my sister, we were sitting outside and shaken with surprise when the voice of the man spoke, again out loud, saying: "call home." I looked at my sister and asked her if she heard that. To which she replied that she had not. I asked her to call home to check on her son and make sure he was okay. Both of us were single parents working hard to make ends meet. She called him and he was fine. Now it was my turn to check on my kids. I called my son and he was fine, then I called my daughter but she was not okay, she had a high fever, and she asked me to come home because she was feeling quite sick.

Is there a higher power looking out for us? Most definitely!!!

I call him God, my Love and my Life. And I'm sure that He loves all of us more than we love Him.

Nothing goes unknown in the eyes of God. He sees and oversees every single thing. Every action, every word, every thought and every reaction. Every deed will count in favour for us or go against us. What we give, we receive. In order to receive good, we have to do good. It will always come back to us, the good will always bring good, and the bad will always bring bad. This is up to us in the choices we make. We have the free will to decide what to do – good or bad.

I know and understand that not everyone believes in God, and I am okay with that. What I have difficulty with is listening to anyone speak poorly of His pure love, of the trust that He entrusted us with, because He knows we are better, we can do better. I know that loving Him and believing in Him is definitely an option that is always available to us.

I encourage people to not speak miserably of something that they refuse to learn about. Do you know God? Have you made the time to create a relationship with Him? A power of Love that encourages us to reflect, to look at ourselves, and to have the courage to change ourselves, to better our ways of living, of caring and of loving.

I'm asking you to be open to something, if not God, something else. Something greater, a higher power of Love where you can find a light, a reassurance, a reason to never give up on your dreams, on your fellow humans, on wanting to create the life you deserve, the desire to heal your hearts, your emotions and to never forget that you belong. You are worthy! You matter!

There's no such thing as we're nothing, or that we're less than anyone else, or that we're not smart enough. None of this exists except in the minds of fear, in the minds that avoid self-reflection, the conflicted minds that cannot see past what they've been taught in this low realm of existence. That is where we are living, a lower dimension, but that is not our essence. We are infinity, multi-dimensional beings, uniting in a Divine completion. And for all that to come to complete manifestation we need to unlearn the old and learn the new.

No God is the wrong God. In fact, His pure Love has created many other Gods to assure that all his children have this pure unconditional

Love available in different places and different cultures, that no child of His will be left unattended. It's okay that your God may have a different face than my God. We must respect them all, including humanity's different choices when they come to select a god of good.

I can tell you that every time we make a choice like that, that very moment we are choosing our higher selves, as we were not created outside of any of His pure Love, but solely from His pure Love.

The Challenging Sea of an Awoken Heart

In every heart there is a God

and in every soul, there is divine,

the whole of all existing life is the light of infinity

in which we are born and rise,

and in which we set and rest in order to start again

The Challenging Sea of an Awoken Heart

Chapter 14

Time Is Divinely Programmed

One of the nights, of the many years I worked two jobs, while driving home I remembered that milk was low in the fridge at home, so I decided to stop by the Seven- Eleven to get milk and a few other things. I stopped, parked the vehicle and went inside. Right behind me this young man also walked in and headed straight to the washroom.

Something was wrong, I could feel it. The clerk seemed upset and started to tell the young man that the washroom was not available. The young man turned around looking very dizzy, and I noticed he was bleeding so much from the side of his face. The clerk seeing the blood demanded him to leave the premises.

It was heart breaking the reality of it all. I spoke up and said that he needed help. I asked for something he could sit on, and I wasn't going to settle for excuses to not help the injured young man. I also asked the clerk for some paper towels, which he said I'd have to pay for.

I said: "I'll pay for it just please bring it me."

I got the young man to sit while I called 911. The other side of the line answered quickly and stayed with me on the phone, helping me help the injured by using paper towels to put pressure on the wound, which was caused by a knife. The ambulance arrived and took the young man to the hospital. Before leaving, the young man thanked me and said that his name was Christopher.

"You are going to fine," I replied, adding a reminder for him to take good care of himself.

I paid for the paper towels and the milk and left to go home.

Synchronicity?? I don't know, but I do know that we're all being watched.

I was happy to get home. My son was playing video games when I walked in the door. I said hi to him and headed straight to the washroom to wash my hands. Seconds after he also came to the washroom where I was still washing my hands. He didn't look ok.

"Are you alright?" I asked.

"No" he said.

He had some upset stomach, but as he was trying to express to me what he was feeling, he fainted and fell hitting his head on the edge of the tub. I went into such a huge panic and started to scream to see if my tenant downstairs could hear me. Kneeling down and holding my boy I was calling his name, but he wasn't waking up. Shortly after, my tenant came in, and I asked him to bring apple juice from the fridge. My son was diabetic and I quickly deciphered he had had a low bad reaction. But deep down I was extremely scared that he had caused huge damage to his head when he fainted and his head hit the bathtub.

You see, the moral of all of this, is that Love loves to love. If I had not helped the young man with the wound in the store, which took a little bit of time, chances were, I'd probably be in bed when my boy fainted. I'd probably be asleep, because I was always overtired. So here I was, back to calling the ambulance a second time in a 20-minute-window. Thank God my son was fine and we went back home. I can't stress enough how important it is to care for others. How important it is to be kind and to take a little bit of our little time to make a difference in other people's lives. One second that is all it takes for everything to change. Good or bad, but that's all it takes.

ALWAYS REMEMBER TO CARE AND TO LOVE

KINDNESS, HUMBLENESS AND MORALS

THAT NO ONE EVER HURTS ANYONE

FOR, EXISTENCE BELONGS TO MORTALS

(Excerpt from "Her Name was Avalon" in Letters to God – my first book)

The Challenging Sea of an Awoken Heart

My life is full of divine and of bliss. It isn't perfect, but I can tell you I am grateful for everything. Even the painful experiences and the hardships, the sacrifices that never got a thank you. The being there for others, when at times I was, in truth, falling apart myself. But I will never forget the ones who were there for me during the most troublesome times in my life.

I am also okay with having made mistakes. For my mistakes gave me the opportunity to look deeper into my darkness, the parts of me that screamed for help. The times that survival was a skill I had to learn at a very young age, that love for others is what helped me survive and thrive. That love gave me reasons to stay alive, to never give up, and to never give in.

No family is perfect and this is a reality of every single family, and that is part of every human life. Life is gift, take it! Embrace it! Take risks and don't take no for an answer. You are here for many reasons and also because the world needs you. Most of all because you need yourself. Would I change anything if I could go back in time? Absolutely not.

The past is in the past, and I'm going to do the best in the now, which is the only reality available to me. Loving the people who love me and pray for the ones that don't love me.

Now if you ask me if people can grow into good people after being raised in hell, after being beaten over and over again, at times that could have caused paralysis, or even brain damage, after being demanded duties that were not meant for children to do, due to the extreme demand of physical labor. Yes, I know people can grow above anything and everything that holds them trapped, being a hostage in fear and despair. People are powerful! In all honesty, many people don't even know the amount of strength they have until being strong is the only option available. Certainly, until they find that strength, that deep desire to remember who they truly are, they will express anger and emotions that really are a scream for help. But with a lot of work, self-love, and also dedicating the time to help others who may need help, also helps heal our own selves.

Trauma is real, anxiety, panic attacks and depression, all this is real, and it is serious but it is treatable in many different ways. I lived through it all, I was housebound for almost a year feeling lost and crippled in it all.

People need to want to get and feel better; people need to believe that they deserve to feel better. People need to stop blaming the past, stop going about it hating and blaming everyone who was in past. Of course, that a lot of it comes from unhealthy homes and unhealthy families, but no amount of blame is going to change anything, no amount of hate is going to heal anyone. And doing to them what they've done to us doesn't make us better than them. It makes us like them. It's a sad reality, isn't it?

I can say that regardless of what I've lived through, I don't hold anything against anyone. I lived and survived hell, but I also know that they also experienced the same hell, but in different ways. They also were raised in hell, they've experienced starvation and extreme poverty while growing up, they didn't have a chance to go to school, didn't have a chance to be children or to play with toys, which was something that was only available to the children of wealthy people. They were exposed to the hard laborious work from sunrise to sunset, many times beneath the stormy and heavy rains or beneath the treacherous heat of the sun. How can we not feel compassion? We have to! We must because that is what makes us whole, that is what leads us to the light that they could never find.

Doing the same. Speaking the same. The judging, hurting, none of it makes us better humans. It only makes us same. Let us forgive, let us lead from the heart. Let us be the people we are meant to be and not what we were thought to be.

God, hear me when I say, please have a safe and loving space in your heavenly home for those who gave us life, those before me and those before them. For only them and you know the hard lives they lived through. As for me, please help me be a better and kinder person every day of my life. Help be aware of my words and of my actions so that I won't hurt anyone or cause a pain that I won't be able to heal.

You are not, and we are not alone. There's always someone who would love to help you, someone who will hug you and assure you that they have got your back. I am that someone, and I know there are many more like me. Don't be afraid to ask. I've got you!

A lyric in a song,

A rustle of sudden warm air,

An embrace of peace, the purest care

A wisp of the winds, heart clouds above,

It's your Angel saying

You are my love

The Challenging Sea of an Awoken Heart

Chapter 15

Alien Encounters

Like many other encounters with human entities and other species, I also have had this amazing encounter with an alien. Hey, that's okay that you shake your head, you have the right to believe it or not! Stuff happens to me. I don't try to make it happen, it just happens when I'm in a quiet state of mind and in a peaceful environment.

Out of body experience, that's exactly what happened again, when I found myself across constellations of endless life. Sometimes I can direct my soul, but sometimes my soul has a mind of its own. So, I really don't put up a fuss! I just let it take me to places I don't remember being before. And as long as I trust and surrender, that it's safe to return home without dying, my soul will lead the way.

The Challenging Sea of an Awoken Heart

Not knowing how it happened, my soul, my body of light, was gliding through the night skies. I could feel the love of its magnificent God and I was delighted with the magic of it all. The pure alignment with my higher self, I remember floating around the stars and smiling at the stars' beauty. They seemed to recognize me, or they knew me, and I felt loved and welcomed. We were, we are a universal family.

Mesmerized, I continued my trip among the stars, and I really didn't want it to ever end. As this beautiful journey continued, I started to hear the sound of playful music. It kind of reminded me the music of a child while jumping in puddles of water. I felt very curious about it, and looking around for something, anything that could make sense of the musical sound, I suddenly saw a being of light. It didn't look like a human being but it did have a form, it was like a see-through body, a body of energy, and it somewhat looked like it was the body of a child alien. This young character really had some amazing personality and he was moving gracefully in between the stars. Gently caressing them with his tiny little hand that looked like it was missing some fingers. "Oh my gosh," I thought, while trying to see its face. It flashed before me for a brief second and then my mind was starting to put words together, "this looks like …" The words were trying to form the sentence: "this looks like an alien," but before I had completed the sentence in my mind, the little alien slid past me like a gentle, fast breeze and with an extremely big, happy smile, he said: "I am an alien." I was speechless. Beyond everything of my greatest understanding, all that I knew was I felt completely in awe with the fact that the alien could clearly transmit my thoughts before I could complete my thinking. I can't remember if I smiled back, but I won't ever forget this encounter. In that moment, he had moved on, but I could still hear the playfulness of the song, and feel his gentleness and his pure love which brought me back into complete unity with God and the whole universe.

We are not alone. I truly believe, especially based on all the experiences I've lived through, that we are surrounded by other species of life. They are of a higher frequency of love and intelligence. They are healers and communicators of higher dimensions and of different worlds, and I believe they will come to us when we're ready to accept them and to embrace them with gratitude and appreciation. Once we are truly ready to evolve and rise above these clouds of doubt, fear, and of judgment in which we humans find such sad comfort, I believe, when that day comes, we humans will be able to see past the illusion of time and separation. When that day comes, if I'm still here on earth, or the other side of life, I will be the first one to bow in gratitude, because that day will be the day that my fellow humans will finally find their freedom, and the love within that unites us all around, all above and below. And therefore, ready to embrace and praise the high Teachers that long to help us in every part of our lives. Some of these Teachers are aliens!

And after all these blessings and miracles, I of course many times find myself face to face with obstacles, also with fears and sometimes extremely hurt by other people, their careless actions, words and ways, and toxic behaviours. I understand that it is the human condition; it is what we've learned versus what we know innately when we're born. What we learn serves leaders of fear. What we were born knowing serves every dimension and its freedom. This is really difficult to be acknowledged by the low vibration of our fearful minds.

In my heart lays the profound pain of watching young lives exiting this world by choice, of witnessing the devastated parents in pain, a kind of pain that never goes away, a death that never ends. My heart drowns in their agony and with the loss of these precious young lives that are so needed for the future of generations to come, because believe me, they will need each other and all the help they can get in order to clean this human mess and reorganize a lot of the earthly files.

Depression, anxiety and panic attacks, this is the most devastating reality of human kind during this time. Many times, I ask myself what has gone wrong? What is it that is missing in their lives? I know that many of these young people come from unhealthy families, from unhappy incidents and some abusive situations, but is that worth taking their own lives? I say, No, not now and not ever! If any of you are going through extreme challenges please speak up, let your needs be heard, let yourself be seen and reminded that you are so loved, that your life is precious, that you are wanted and needed, that no one can replace you. Please have compassion for yourself and for your families and friends too, regardless of the wrong done to you. You have the power to overcome, you have the power to heal, and you have a duty to your own life and the obligation to keep your life safe. I know that being young is complicated and sometimes you may feel lost and helpless, but I promise you that healing and rising above the turmoil of life is possible, and I'm here to help you remember that.

No one is perfect and everyone is going through some hardship that no one else knows about. Every single person cries many times in the darkness of their pain and fears, but to think of taking your precious life is not the way to live, and most definitely never ever the way to die.

With everything that's going on, I think of all the people fighting life-threatening illnesses, hoping to be able to survive and to be given the chance to live a little longer. I think of the people going through dialysis day after day, week after week, month after month, and year after year, waiting and praying for a transplant, the people stuck in wheelchairs, and many others confined to a bed. What a sad reality to watch and witness their anxieties about the unknown, and their unpredictable future, even if they will live long enough to have one. But they still try to live with some faith that they will get better, they look for that little light of hope at the end of a turbulent night, for those first rays of light in the very early morning, the awakening of a new day that brings light to their lives. That sadly some of them can only see it from the inside of their hospital room.

I cannot stress enough the fact that you, young generation of Earth, are the blessings and the miracles of this time on our planet. You have been called for great things, but are also being tested with great challenges and courage. You've been called and chosen by God and the universe to assist and to lead the ascension of humanity. You cannot let go of you and cannot let go of each other. Please take responsibility for yourself and rethink your decisions!

The Challenging Sea of an Awoken Heart

You, young people, are in my heart, and your beautiful heart beats matter to me, and to your loved ones. I don't know if you believe in God, but He believes in you. He loves you and would love to see you through your darkest moments with His Divine Light. Please ask for help and please embrace the help. Remember that you are not alone.

I come from nowhere to hide for safety, nowhere to go, no one that could understand me and no one that could help me. Honestly, it's my love for others, the deep desire to keep them safe that gave me the strength to never give up, that gave me the courage to never stop fighting for what I believed in. I looked for ways that could help me grow above the heights of the loneliness and the beauty of a small island in the middle of the Atlantic Ocean. The more I read and the farther I looked passed the oceans of uncertainty, the farther away I could see. I loved the vision, deep down believing that there was so much more. There was and still is. As difficult as it has been at times, I'm loving the journey and I wish that I can help everyone love theirs.

Life is precious, and in my every waking first moment of the morning, I light a candle and ask God to keep my children, my family, and my friends looked after, in health, in happiness, and in peace. I ask God to help the children of the Earth and to give them courage to never give up regardless of what they're going through. The strength to endure knowing that God is a master at the impossible, that He is the Light during the darkest times and the Love that never let's go. All God asks from us is to believe. So simple, isn't it?

Living and experiencing, it truly is a beautiful opportunity to perfect ourselves and to reflect and choose to be a better, more compassionate, and kind person. Not just to others but also to ourselves. To hold in our hearts that loves loving and in our souls that light that never goes out, and that helps us see through the darkest moments we all sometimes endure.

To be human is difficult. To be human means emotion, and emotions, if not dealt with especially when it is of low frequency, can create and recreate monsters. They can destroy everything that they come in contact with, they can blind the faith and the light that our souls are born with, the gift of eternal life that our physical and mental bodies need in order to exist in this lower dimension. Emotions can be of high and happy vibration, but when they are low and negative, they can become monsters and certainly our worst enemies. We must learn to tame the beasts! We must recognize the amount of pain and distress they cause and how those low frequencies can affect our lives. If we don't deal with them, we will get sick and eventually we will project the same low vibration and energy onto our loved ones. We would unknowingly hurt them and cause pain that sometimes can never be repaired, healed or fixed. The truth is that I've learned this deep awareness of pain, the kind of pain that breaks the heart and sometimes injures our soul. I've learned about the pain from getting hurt by the people I loved and trusted the most. To be human is to be constantly challenged by everything that we're not, and to master one emotion after the other. To learn to say no to anything and everything that may not be a loving invitation, to say no to everything that no longer holds our highest good. To honour ourselves and the divine within that constantly tries to remind us that we are so much better, that only by acknowledging our divine can we become aligned with the all-encompassing Love of God, that only by learning the power of Love can we rise above all that holds us back from being our highest selves.

We cannot change other people but we can change ourselves, and that is one of the most important things we have been assigned with. The responsibility for ourselves and accountability for all we do. This is the only way to heal the emotion of blame, and to heal the need to judge or condemn our fellow humans, this is the way to free ourselves and the way to give ourselves permission to rise above all emotional clouds that block us from our divine light. Yes, we are that light, that often we turn it off because we resist changes, and resist letting go of what we've learned. Not only the constricted teachings that we've been subjected to, but everything that keeps us small and blended with everything we are not, and everything we don't believe in. As long we give into fear, we will live in fear, as long we live in condemnation, we will live in fear of being condemned, as long as we give energy to hate we will live looking for something to hate or to be unhappy about and also feeling that people hate us. Our mind is a trap and will trap everything we feed to it. Our minds can either be our best friend or our worst enemy. Everything is going to depend on how well we master one emotion after the other.

IF ONLY TO LEARN THIS DIVINE LOVE, WAS I BORN ON EARTH, THAT WOULD BE SO MUCH MORE THAN ANYTHING I COULD EVER ASK FOR

The Challenging Sea of an Awoken Heart

Be gentle with yourself. Don't allow challenges, disappointments, heart breaks, or adversity to define who you are. You are powerful, and as long you breathe, walk, and talk, you have the power to choose. You may be a sheep without a shepherd, but I assure you that there is a shepherd always waiting to love you and to be loved, to guide you, and to hold you during the most troubled times of life. You may not find Him in church or religious societies, because unfortunately they are very selective when it comes to opening the doors to all of humanity. God is a shepherd and you can find Him anywhere; in the woods, in the middle of corn fields, or simply by sitting on the beach counting the grains of sand.

I was a very young girl when all around me was chaos, threats, and being filled with fear and uncertainty. Every minute of my life, since I can remember to about 12 or 13 years old, was filled with stress and with anxiety. I slept very little; always sleeping lightly and listening to every sound, because around 2AM or 3AM in the morning the loving devil in my life would wake up half sober and half drunk and that was the most dangerous time of the night. He would be screaming or throwing things, calling my mother names, and then in a panic Mom would try to calm him down to dreadfully be physically attacked. That was always the most painful thing for me to watch, because it didn't matter how scared I was, I always interfered, I always tried to protect her and beg Dad to not do it or to stop. Sometimes I was successful and other times I would be flying across the room.

"Oh well! I guess I became pretty good at the craft." No, it's not funny, but as long as I smile upon remembering those hardships, I believe I heal my heart and my soul.

I hated when my little sisters would wake up to that misery and that my brother Jamie, who was so deeply sensitive, would wake with full panic in his face, and I could see the intense fear in his eyes. I hated being a tiny and completely helpless little young human. I didn't have the size or the strength to chain up this by-alcohol-possessed man, and I despise that I couldn't change that reality. Many times, I wished that I was one of my elder brothers because they were older and stronger, and many times I wished they had the courage to interfere, to stop that infernal agony. But they didn't, and I don't judge them, because I understand that they probably were scared too of the same thing that I was seeing. Maybe they were afraid of causing damage that would not be possible to repair. I honestly don't know, but I do know that the man I loved so much was lucky that I was not one of his eldest sons. Deep down I never really wanted to hurt him, it was never about revenge, it was all about tying him up while sobering up, so he could no longer hurt Mom or any of us. Immobilize the devil that was running through his veins; the alcohol.

All of that lasted until I was about twelve years old, because on that day my father stopped drinking and never again touched a drop of alcohol. I am to this present day grateful for that because deep down my father was not a monster. In fact, he was a good man with a great big heart, filled with love and with compassion. The alcohol was the monster, not him, and when he stopped drinking the monster was gone. That's when his true nature would be fully present; he was peaceful, loving and so safe to be with.

Sadly, there was still so much physical abuse beneath our leaky roof, so unpredictable, so silent and so demonic. I remember the pain in my stomach, it was filled with nervousness and anxiety, and the complete dark fear of it all when I watched that one person walk towards me like he was on a mission to kill. Every time this happened, I felt I died a little bit more inside. The beating was so horrible and the kicking of those boots were unbearable, leaving my little body battled with bruises and my head left with bumps. I was in so much pain for days to follow, but nobody knew because I was afraid of speaking up, and because I knew if I did, the next time would be worse. Was that person a happy person? I believe not! Happy people don't hurt people. Sometimes I wonder what kind of devils had he encountered while growing up? Which part of his miserable existence was he stuck in that kept him a prisoner of his heart and a shadow on his light?

The Challenging Sea of an Awoken Heart

My mother, the woman I so loved and hurt deeply for her pain, she was so broken and so lost. She too didn't have an idea of her actions, of how much her loving heart was consumed by hate and fear. Her sudden changes of emotions and behaviour could never be predicted, and I was the one who paid the price for that during many different times of anger attacks. Eventually when I was around thirteen years old, I finally gained the courage to confront her. I vividly remember this episode and perhaps it was the last one. She was heating up the large concrete oven with wood, located in the wall of our kitchen, this was the way to make a lot of bread. The oven could bake 13 or 14 big breads each time, and the truth is that we needed it because we had a house full of people. She told me to go outside and get the long and thick stick that she usually used to move the firewood around inside the oven, and so I brought it inside the kitchen. I placed it standing up against a corner and I honestly don't remember exactly what followed and what it was that made her so angry at me, I only remember her being so outraged that she picked up the stick and walked towards me with a frightening look on her face, a look that said that she was going to kill me with that stick. I believe she meant it, and I was frightened as no one could believe, but I couldn't move or run for my life anymore, and I didn't want to. I don't really know what happened, but as she was going to start, she raised her arm with the stick.

I said to her: "go ahead and do it, but only if it heals your misery, only if it will make you feel better or happier. Or if it will help you become a better person."

I stood there not knowing what would happen next. Not knowing if the next moment would be death or freedom. She stood there ready to hit the target but she couldn't, and throwing the stick in the corner, she walked away. From then on, she never hurt me again. In fact, we started to have a closer relationship and understanding of each other, and in time even shared some good conversations and laughs. I saw a transformed woman. However, deep down there was a woman lost in pain and remorse. She was a woman that had endured a life of grief for losing her three babies and broken by all the abuse and the hard life she lived. She was a woman that deserved to be loved and to be reminded that she was worthy and beautiful, but nobody bothered to tell her those beautiful things, or to hug her and tell her thank you for everything that she did while raising a big family with so little food to set on the table. There, right there, I promised myself that I would live to encourage and empower women to free themselves from all the chains of abuse, and of controlling personalities. In memory of my mother, I have done that, and I will continue to stand for the rights of women. Not only that, but I will stand with them, speak with them and for them.

NOT ONE DAY IS SAME AS THE OTHER, WHY WOULD WE STAY SAME

The Challenging Sea of an Awoken Heart

Nothing is going to change unless we change the way we look at things and at life itself. Old ways don't pave new ways. The only way is love, and only to love it is fully worth living. My soul is my divine temple of love and of peace, of that eternal knowing that I so seek to remember. Our souls are filled with memories, files of information from past lives and from higher dimensions of infinite love, light, and wisdom.

Unfortunately, from the moment we're born, we humans start being marinated and brain-washed by earthly concepts. Concepts taught to us by families, societies and religions, and also by different cultures, their beliefs and their ways. In order to fit into this low vibrational dimension, we are taught to learn the vibration of time and limitations. All kinds of beliefs and congregations working on separating us from the divine within ourselves. Which leaves people blinded by the needs of being accepted, and blinded by the desire to belong, yet fall prey to systematic systems. Sadly, many of them will follow without question everything they don't believe in, just to fit in. This leaves us with the loss of the very power we need to make the necessary change; the courage, the strength, the freedom that was taken away from us, the right of speech and the right to speak the truth, which is so simple, and the right to live with dignity.

The Challenging Sea of an Awoken Heart

Whatever it is you're following,

Whether it's religion or set of beliefs,

If they don't inspire you

To be a better person

Then you're following the wrong ones.

The Challenging Sea of an Awoken Heart

Chapter 16

The Gift And The Curse

My prophetic dreams; the gift and the curse. Yes, they are that! And yet, I cannot change that, nor would I want to. It is part of my life and my journey on Earth. These dreams are never about happy upcoming events, unfortunately. They are always about tragedies, losses, and grief. This particular one, was sometime during the late summer of 1986. In my dream I was sitting on the couch in my living room. The couch faced the glass sliding door, and outside was the beautiful garden. I could also see the traffic passing by, back and forth, on Argyle Street in Vancouver, the beauty of the flowers, and watching life happening out there, when suddenly, I couldn't help but notice a hurst pulling over outside the front yard. I felt kind of worried and stood up to get closer to the glass sliding doors to see if that hurst was really for me. In getting closer I could see my father and my sister, Lucia, sitting in the front. In my dream, I started to cry and saying: "oh no my mother passed away!" In that moment I awoke with a shock and was already crying. I felt as if fear was choking me with tears of such a scary and vivid nightmare. Eventually I calmed down and went back to sleep when I had the realization that this couldn't be, because on the Island they didn't use hursts to deliver the deceased. On the Island it used to be a funeral procession to carry the coffin from the house to the church, and then from the church to the cemetery, followed by family and friends. With that in mind I somehow felt at peace, dismissing the dream as a very unpleasant and scary meeting.

Some months passed after I had this dream, and I was not informed that my mother was very sick. I had been in a difficult pregnancy and my family didn't want to upset me. After I had my baby girl, my first born, I was informed that my mother was in the hospital. The doctors didn't know what was wrong with her, but they kept medicating her. She was treated for so many issues that she didn't have, including her heart. Finally, after months of poisoning the patient with wrong medications, and close to the end of the year, her fever was so high and in no way would come down. The hospital on Saõ Jorge called another Island's hospital, one that was so much more advanced with the medical knowledge and quality care. They sent a helicopter to go pick my mother up by emergency, and my father went with her. When they landed outside the hospital on Terceira Island, the ambulance was waiting and she was assisted right of way. My father was lost and scared while waiting, and he realized that this was bad. It was not until the doctor came to see him and told him that my mother had a kidney infection, that if treated in time she would've been fine. Since too much time had passed there was nothing he could do; the infection had spread and her fever was completely out of control. I was told she was in excruciating pain. The entire third floor of the hospital could hear her agony and laments. My mother was mostly delirious with the fever and she wasn't aware of what was happening, but she'd have those moments here and there, that she would tell the nurses that she had children, and one of the daughters was living in Canada. She continuously would beg the doctors to not let her die, to be saved. My brother Joe and sister Lucia followed them to Terceira Island to be with our father and mother. Eventually after a few days my brother left and my sister stayed with our father. It was there that my mother passed away. That was the very first time I've experienced the devastation of grief. I was so far away and there was nothing I could do. I couldn't hold my mom, and I couldn't tell her how much I Loved her in her final moments. There on the island of Terceira they had the hurst and that was the transportation used to deliver her to her last home. Exactly like the dream. The dream wasn't just a dream, it was a nightmare meeting with the future. It was the reality of the near future arriving with degrading pain. It took me years to let go, to heal the desire of bombing the hospital, of the spite I held towards the hospital. My rage was towards the doctors and the staff that misdiagnosed and treated her with the wrong narcotics for several months. They destroyed her health and took her away from her family, including the children, who were still so young and who needed her so much.

But life goes on, right? It has to. Some people say we don't have a choice but to keep on living, but we do have a choice. In all honesty, I don't have a memory of being dead, but I know that being alive while learning to live again, it is extremely painful, every minute of our reality. As time passed, I learned with every passing day that every day without her was another day closer to being with her, and that bathed my heart with hope.

I FELT YOUR KISS, I'VE HEARD YOUR SONG

PLEASE KNOW I LOVE YOU,

I KNOW WE WILL MEET AGAIN, AS I GO ALONG

(Excerpt from "Roses for Momma" in Letters to God – my first book)

The Challenging Sea of an Awoken Heart

Prophetic dreams or hunting dreams. I don't really know what to call them. They leave me filled with anxiety and fear, especially because many of them do happen in real life. This one was a few months after my mother passed away. As always it was vivid and real. In this dream, I was walking in a long field. There was nothing special to it except as I was enjoying my walk, I realized the figure, a short distance away, was my father. It looked like he was sitting on the grass. I thought that was strange but kept on walking towards him. When I got close to him, I noticed that he was sitting with his legs hanging inside an open grave. He was playfully swinging his legs from side to side inside this grave. I felt petrified with what I was seeing. I hesitantly asked him what was he doing there. Then added softly to it for him to get out of there. He lifted his eyes and looked at me with a faint smile, then he said, "don't worry about me. I'm okay but I promised your mother that I would go to be with her."

I woke up from this hunting nightmare shaking and so very upset with the possibility of losing my other parent, or what the unknown near future would be. I was afraid of his life coming to end, especially after seeing my mother's funeral in one of these dreams a few months prior to her passing.

The devastating reality is that he passed away 11 months after mother, and about 6 months after my prophetic dream. As much it was so painful for me to lose my father, I knew in my heart that they belonged together, and together from up there, they would watch over us.

No, I couldn't and didn't have the right to be selfish, or to judge my father in his pain and his grief. Or even with his passing. He loved us so much. His children were everything he loved the most, but life was done with him, and unfortunately, with having a stroke, God helped him get home maybe a little sooner than he had planned. I know he would've endured a life of sacrifice and even one filled with pain, but I know he wouldn't want to leave his children as soon as he did. That dream was his sweet and kind heart preparing me to be strong, for me and my siblings. I am grateful to be the daughter of this man that had the courage to abandon the evil, vicious addiction of alcohol for the love he had for us. It was with him I learned the most profound and the most beautiful and simplest truths about humbleness and kindness, but most of all a life about being a good human. With my father I learned to never give up on anything and everything that was important to me.

SO MANY YEARS HAD COME AND GONE,

MUCH OF HIS LOVE, HIS WORDS I REMEMBER EVERY DAY,

BUT MISSING YOU FATHER, STILL IS SO PROFOUND.

ADEUS PAI, EU TE AMO FILHA,

WE WILL MEET ALONG HEAVEN'S HIGHWAY

(Excerpt from "My Father and I, Our Last Goodbye" from the second Letters to God – my next book)

The Challenging Sea of an Awoken Heart

My prophetic dreams and the amount of grief they brought into my living life. Often the fear and the uncertainty of what would be next, along with my desperation and anxieties with being hunted by this living phantom along my lonely different roads. It is the price for being different or weird, whatever people call it, it is my reality and as real as every breath I take. I cannot change this. I cannot hide from it. And I cannot change the awareness that it is part of my life on Earth, of my walk-through life, and of my destiny. Similar to the fact that I cannot change the truth that the voice is the son of man and when it calls it yells because it needs to be heard and doesn't leave room for options.

ITS VIBRATIONS FILLED MY HOME,

IT WAS HEAVEN'S MAILMAN.

CLEAR AND LOUD SAYING

THAT, THE VOICE WAS THE SON OF MAN

(Excerpt from "introductions" in Letters to God – my first book)

The Challenging Sea of an Awoken Heart

Next, and this I know, is very profound, to a certain extent, but weighs heavy on my heart and soul. In fact, it involves so much more than one person or a family member, or a friend, or even anyone of concern. It makes me feel like I carry the weight of the world on my shoulders. It is a greater concern for the safety of humanity in general.

It was the summer of the year 2016. Again, this was a dream, and in this dream, I was somewhere that I didn't recognize. I was inside a small room, dimly lit, and I was by myself. Shortly after I realized that, I could hear people talking on the other side of the wall. It must be in the room next to me, I thought. There were voices of men talking, and somehow it felt like the topic of conversation was of a serious matter. I tried to hear what the conversation was about, but after a few attempts I understood that it would be almost impossible to hear through the wall. I asked, out loud, what was happening, having the faith that they would answer me, but to my complete surprise the answer came from the same voice I had heard before. I recognized it, but I had not heard it in a dream before. Previously, it had been during events in my awake-life, during my day-to-day duties. This time that same voice spoke in my dream, and this time that same voice responded to my question in a tone of disbelief.

It said: "how don't you know? It is an Earthquake, and it is a big one! It has been programmed, and it will happen December 13."

With this statement, I woke up shaking and feeling traumatized. I was filled with anxiety. My racing heart wouldn't calm, but in my mind, there was a question looming. What do I do? What should I do? Should I say something or should I stay quiet? Such turmoil I felt inside. I discussed it with some family members, and they had concerns about sharing it with the media. They were worried about my well-being. Of course, they would support me with any decision I'd make. After some months of feeling lost and uncertain, and with the month of December approaching, my anxiety was also trying to engulf me in misery. I'd ask myself so many times, what could be worse? Sharing it with the media and the possibility of nothing happening, being made to look like a fool, or staying quiet with the possibility that it could happen. What could be worse? Having my liver being chewed alive by the media if it didn't happen, or living the remainder of my life filled with remorse and guilt if it did happen and I didn't try to warn people, so that they could prepare and stay safe.

I felt conflicted and stuck between a rock and a hard place. I decided it was important to share and for people to know regardless what would come my way. I chose to share it with social media, while trying hard to prepare myself for whatever nasty behaviour would come towards me. In my heart at any moment of my life I'd prefer to be wrong rather than to watch people lose their lives, knowing that it could've been prevented by calling for safety. As we all now know nothing happened. Yes, I did get treated poorly and endured much abusive rhetoric online by those who were disappointed that it didn't happen. But I will not forget, there were people that stood by me and stood up for me. I am grateful for the ones who loved me and understood the courage and love that it took for me to expose my heart and my soul for the good of others. It took many months for self-care to shake it off.

However, based on the many years of experiencing the devastating outcomes of my prophetic dreams, I believe it will happen. I just don't know the year because it wasn't given to me, but it will be on a December 13. And because I live in Vancouver, I believe the message is for the surrounding area where I live. Which means it would happen along the fault line close to Vancouver, Vancouver Island, Seattle, Washington, and Portland, Oregon, and so on. However, it may or may not be while I'm here on earth, but I have no doubt that it will happen because that voice does not lie. That voice has guided me through many difficult times of my life, and it has saved me and my sister on the highway.

Life goes on and life passes by in the blink of an eye. You're in it and you no longer are. Like time, you have it but you don't. What a beautiful miracle of life this is, and with it we are given the opportunity to be living life here on Earth. This gift comes with many opportunities to grow and to learn, to make better choices every day, about ourselves and all that surrounds us. To watch the perfection of a drop of water, and to see how gracefully a plant grows; all so perfectly programmed, and yet with a mind of its own to learn and choose. Everything knows what to do in order to be. How fascinating it is to watch the movement of the clouds and its divine shapes, all that reminds us that life does exist in higher realms of existence. The beautiful rising and setting of the sun all over the Earth at different times, so that every living being gets to witness the divine waking and the divine resting. The portraying of infinite life that never let's go, and with it, the deep understanding of how our beautiful universe has been so perfectly created. The endless life that so perfectly has been programmed and timed. Every small atom and particle are an intelligent matter, not the internet intelligence as we have come to rely on, but a before time ancient intelligence. Every seed is programmed. How could one not be humbled by the Creator that created everything that we are, all that we touch and see. The visible and the invisible, which is all visible for those who believe and want to see, and real in the many different dimensions of life along our infinite constellations. I don't know how you feel about it but I myself live in a deep end of appreciation, and this is a place that I pray to never ever let go, because it's here, in this awareness, that I came to know the divine within myself. That divine is within every individual and every living being. And that's where I come to greet you all.

No separation, and no better or worse, no richer or poorer, all this branded information is an illusion of time, a conspiracy belief that fills the void of a much more profound and deeper understanding. In all honesty, it saddens me very much because I watch the suffering and the struggles that people live through. They live in a desperation to be what they are not, to follow what they don't really believe in, and to be a profile they are not and don't honour. How devastating, the energy being used and the time being wasted to harm one another. Sadly, a life poorly lived is worse than being dead.

It's unfortunate that human history repeats itself over and over again. The crime continues and many times by the people who are supposed to keep civilians safe. Yes, the judgment continues and many times by misplaced "your honours" without honour. Yes, the slavery continues with many people being underpaid and the rich getting richer from paying their employees the lowest wages. Yes, discrimination still happens every day and everywhere, and I myself have witnessed it even in schools by teachers and principals. All in all, every decision is a choice with a ticket-to-kill-power-trippers and bullies. The people who abuse their positions in society. And as much as I am filled with empathy and work hard to practice forgiveness, the stupidity of humanity keeps growing in a very alarming way. I feel that as long as we watch the crime happen without trying to stop it, we are just as criminal; as long as we watch the abuse happen, without protecting the victims, we become the abusers. Silence is killing. We need to come together and join for the right of speaking up and being heard, and for the freedom of all people that are being held under the thumb; the freedom of all the people who's right of speech has been taken away. It's time to stand up against the "justice" that is shooting innocent people, that is silencing the truth, that is inflicting pure fear in civilians instead of keeping them safe. To my awareness it's heart-braking, that part of our hard-earned taxes is used to pay towards a system that is supposed to keep people safe. Who needs enemies when you have a system like this?

AS LONG AS WE LAY LOW AND STAY QUIET, THE SICK SYSTEMS WILL STAND HIGHER.

The Challenging Sea of an Awoken Heart

It's addicting, the desire to blame, the lack of accountability and of integrity. And this goes into religious systems and how they use God to condemn, to judge, to kill, to rape, and to create wars. All in the name of God. Have they forgotten that God gave His son's life to teach forgiveness? Have they forgotten that God assisted the poor and the homeless? Have they forgotten that God asked to protect the children and the innocent? What the hell is wrong with organized religious societies that commit all kinds of everything evil in the name of God? Yet they are never at fault. As they say, they represent God, but fail to open the doors to the homeless, to the helpless, to the injured, and to the starving; to the sheep without a shepherd. And then I come to think of how selfish I am when I think of God giving the life of His only Son to teach His Children forgiveness, gifting them with eternal Life. I wouldn't give my children's lives to teach anyone a damn thing! And yes, you can call me selfish, but so are you, because you too would not give the life of what you love the most. But God did, so stop the blame. And start taking accountability and living a truth that benefits everyone, and doesn't leave anyone in the cold of the winter or beneath the heat of the sun.

A criminal, some people call God a criminal, and yet they haven't taken a minute to get to know Him. They haven't taken a minute of silence to be able to hear Him. They haven't taken a minute of quiet to let him talk. Species of little faith, fully committed to hate, fully committed to fear, and fully committed to be everything they are not.

But anyways, how can one get to know God if it doesn't know itself? How can one be committed to Love if they focus on hate? Honestly there is no room for the two. In order to love you have to dismiss all that is not Love.

And in all honest truth, and in my love-to-love deepest desire, I ask that if you've lost your way to your own self then you need to retrace your steps, and start over. No, you don't need to go and read and re-read the Bible over and over again from the beginning to the end. Remember, God is the Bible! But not everything that is in the Bible is

God's creation. Much of it in truth, just like the church, is man-made, dressed in rich gowns and regalia. They are organized societies of fear that grow their power over people's weaknesses, anxieties, and poverty, over people's silence, over people's bank accounts, over people's fears. And then comes Hell in all its glory! Again, people have forgotten why God has given His only Son's Life; and they brake God's rules over and over again, and bleach its Truth with all kinds of sins and lies. Hell is a state of mind, decorated with illness, with fear, with darkness, and all kinds of evil deeds. So, hell is on Earth, not anywhere up there by the stars. So be good to you, be good to everyone that seeks you. Help all you can! And if you cannot help, then do nothing, go home quietly and better yourself in the aspects that you think you need the most. After all, time is all we have and all that we don't. Let's make us better people! Let's love us a little more so that we can better love others. Let's forgive others so that we may be forgiven. And if you don't know God, I encourage that you may seek Him, for God is real. He is your heart and in every little thing that surrounds you.

No one gets out of Earth alive. Fortunately, we all have arrived with the ticket to return. In a grave yard it doesn't matter who's richer, who's the most important, in a grave yard everyone is same, just like in the waiting rooms of every ICU. It won't matter what we own. It will only matter the love we share, how we care for others during our own tragedies, the hugs we give when people need one and the reminder that no one is alone. The encouragement to never give up. I truly wish people could understand simple truths, understand the divine within themselves, and find a way of never losing that sacred space.

I cannot change anyone. I wouldn't want to change anyone, as I understand every single person is here to live their own lives, to walk their own journey, and to learn their own lessons. Which in fact is not a sin, they are not sins. They are opportunities to learn to grow and to glow. Can I fully make sense of every lesson of my life? No, I cannot, but I know that for everything there is a reason, and I myself want that reason to be an opportunity to become a better person. I pray that I never let go of this light that illuminates my path, and my faith in God, and in humanity, that will always lead my life and help me help those who seek help. We have to care for each other, care for the less fortunate, and sometimes it only takes a smile and a reminder that they are not alone and that they do matter.

We never know when it is the last minute we have here, the last breath we take, the last heartbeat. Everything is unknown. In truth we are living in borrowed time. This is not ours to keep. But of course, when we are healthy, many of us don't see or think of the end of the line, the last step we take, the last word we say. But I know that it only takes one second for it all to end. One second that is all it takes for everything to change forever, and that not only the elderly and the sick die, unfortunately, the graveyard is full of young and of healthy people. Many didn't have the time to live and to experience this amazing earthly school, so when I think of me and of the many others that are being gifted with the time for being here, I feel what a blessing to have the opportunity to choose to be a good person, to help others remember the good in themselves. What a dream come true to live a long life, a life of learning to be better, and a chance to break the rules of any teaching that teaches us differently.

So, enjoy this time, your time. Don't waist it with pity little insignificant things. One day it will all be history. Write an awesome story and once in a while don't be afraid of editing if you must, because one day someone will tell stories about you. Make it worthy of sharing because your story may become the strength of someone feeling weak, it may be the light of someone lost in the darkness, it may be the faith of someone who may be thinking of giving up or quitting. That day you may not be here to hear your stories, but the memories of the love you leave behind will echo through the heavens, and the inspiration you've shared can help others find their own strength and the courage to never let go of their dreams and desires.

Divine signs and divine presence, I believe many of us have experienced these phenomenal miracles. Many of us have acknowledged its true reality and many of us have dismissed it, as it was probably just imagination. I have been so blessed with the signs during extreme turbulent times in my life. I'd like to share it with you and remind you that regardless of your beliefs and, or religious backgrounds, you are never alone, you are not unworthy, and you are a child of God. He loves you regardless of the wrongs you've done!

Without any deep detail and with so much respect and love to the person that has endured the fear of the unknown next day, or if there would be a next one.

The Challenging Sea of an Awoken Heart

May you find strength

During difficult times.

Courage when needing to

Make hard decisions.

Light throughout the clouds of fear and doubt,

May you find love and peace

In every decision you make.

The Challenging Sea of an Awoken Heart

Chapter 17

Miracles In White

My phone rang, and a soft voice spoke on the other end with the request for me to sit down. Well right there my heart skipped a beat. With my knees trembling I carefully took a seat. With kindness, I was informed of very sad news about someone I love with all my heart; that someone on the other end of the line was crying and feeling very scared and very lost. There was a possibility of a long wait for an organ, an organ???? Oh my god! What had happened?

In my heart there were many questions that I couldn't ask, but I so wanted to be that donor. Yet because of my heart condition, doctors wouldn't even look at me. What should I do? I drove to go see this amazing person, who's fate never failed to be tested by faith in every possible way during this person's life. I got there and the three of us hugged and cried, and I asked them to have faith. Yes, faith was so much needed, and a donor too.

Days and weeks followed by months, it all passed by slowly and filled the air with so much fear and anxiety. I was failing the faith in myself; sometimes the fears would block the light of my path and my trust that somehow it would all work out. And that was when I had to shout God's name, just to make sure that He was still having my back. Morning hours were filled with pacing back and forth, crying and asking God to give me a sign that all would be okay.

"Help me help this large piece of my heart," I prayed.

It was during one of those mornings, a late summer morning, that something unexplainable took place. It was a little cloudy outside, and I was feeling as sad as I probably looked. Like every morning I was home alone. I could hear my second coffee brewing while I was pacing and talking to God and the angels, with the tears flowing from my sleepless eyes and bathing my aging cheeks. When suddenly something on the outside of the large bay windows of the kitchen got my attention. It didn't look so cloudy anymore, if anything, it looked like it was snowing. Impossible! I thought, this could not be. I walked to the window to take a closer look I could not understand what was happening. Snow? I had to blink a couple of times and look away, but no, it wasn't snow. Whatever it was, there was so much of it, and in beautiful pure white. I decided to go outside and check it out for myself. I was flabbergasted and couldn't believe what my eyes were seeing. There was the most beautiful thing happening in a way that could not be imagined. It wasn't snow, it was thousands of white feathers, slowly falling from the skies. To make it even more unbelievable, it was only covering our driveway, from the outside of the property entrance gates to the very end of the driveway. There were no feathers on the back yard or front yard, neither on the side of the driveway, nor outside of the gates or on the road. I was speechless, and in actuality, I can't even find the words to fully express this magical love. This divine sign that was happening was from Heaven and from its Messengers of eternal Love. I stood there with my hands open beneath that Heaven and repeatedly said: "Thank you to God and the angels." That moment, deep in my heart, I knew that God was on the wheel of my ship, and that my passenger would be okay. I knew that my prayers were being answered. And I knew that God is good, oh soooo good! Again, my Lord and my heavenly King, I thank you for all of the miracles and the love that you have granted me and my loved ones during this time on Earth.

Just in case you may be thinking of dead birds, nope, not a chance! There wasn't a single dead bird.

After all the magic settled, and filled with gratitude and happiness, I called my husband at work and told him about what had taken place outside. I bet he was kind of like, 'okay whatever,' but saying: "Wow honey, that's amazing! We'll talk later."

He quickly went back to work. When he arrived at home from work around 4PM that day, I didn't see him arrive, for whatever reason, and when I realized that he had arrived, I saw that he was walking around the driveway and looking at the many feathers that were still laying on the grounds. When I came outside and stood next to him, nothing was said, no comments were added. We looked at each other and knew that something extremely divine had happened. I understood the language of silence and was grateful that he too could now fully understand the divine I could see, and the pertinent role it plays in my life.

THE BEGINNING IS NOT THE END, THE END IS THE BEGINNING

The Challenging Sea of an Awoken Heart

My life has been a whirl-wind of so many challenges, and of hard work. But to start with, I love the wind. He is my friend. With it come the opportunities for me to change directions. To go with it or to go against it. It always depends on what's in it, not just for me but for others too. Its magic is persuasion and certainly caresses in ways that nothing else can.

Some of my storms are written here in this set of life lessons and adventures. But so are the many rainbows of my life and my soul. And the many rainfalls that washed away all the tears I couldn't get rid of. I can now fully understand the meaning and the purpose of every person in my life, regardless if they were blood related or not. Every single life played the role of magic in my existence, every single love was a love I needed to experience in order to learn love. Meaning, the love I am and the love I am capable of being. The love that frees instead of the love that holds back. The love that expands instead of love that constricts. But most definitely a love that says: "Hey! Wait for your turn." For this moment right now it's Maria's turn. My turn. Yes, it took me a long time to learn to love myself. It took me a long time to learn that I no longer had any obligation of carrying around the guilt of other people's doings. Their behaviour was still the same but it no longer affected me in any way, and that doesn't mean that the blame had stopped. Not at all. Unfortunately, the blame and the insulting still are some people's way of unloading their lack of growth and accountability. It's sad to watch so much hate, so much greed, control and ignorance. But I understand it's something that they must master on their own in order to free themselves from themselves. And sometimes, a reality will hit them right where it hurts, over and over again until reflection finally shows them their hearts and souls, instead of their malicious and calculated, controlling minds, and unhappy existence.

I am deeply grateful that God gives me the courage and the wisdom to finally let go of the people and the situations that no longer hold my highest good at heart, and that regardless of the amount of good I've done, and still do, they'll never learn the meaning of appreciation. Takers are not givers, they are takers. And that's what they'll always be. That for me is a space I refuse to embrace, and it's an emptiness, a void that I refuse to fulfill. It's not my job, it's for them to learn and choose to change in order to better themselves.

The Challenging Sea of an Awoken Heart

Chapter 18

Good People Go To Bars Too

I'd love to share with you all that I did find the love of my life. My twin flame and my great friend. My man of my many past lives. Terrance and I met at the beginning of 2017. And since then, we've always been together. We've grown a little older together, we've travelled quite a bit together, and we've built all we could together. Just for giggles and some laughs, I'm going to share with you, how we met. To start, I used to say, I'd never ever date someone I'd meet in a bar. You probably know why – bar, alcohol, memories, and all the red flags screaming, 'stay safe!'

It was the evening of March 11th, when I received a phone call from a friend of mine, who was also my son's friend. He invited me to get together at Sam's Pub in Langley. He told me that my son and his wife would be joining us too. I was tired and not really in the mood for the drive, and I guess he could sense my hesitation, as he added, that he had a friend that he would like for me to meet. Saying that we had so much in common. Wow, I thought, a boyfriend?? I didn't want one. Not close by, not far away, and not nowhere. As I, truthfully speaking, was focusing on healing from a horrible experience I had just left behind a few months prior. That person was the biggest narcissist I've ever met in my life. That individual spoke a few different languages but never knew the language of love and respect. He kept losing one good woman after the other because he could not succeed at breaking them to his liking.

Anyway, still with my friend on the phone, I ended up agreeing to meet while reminding myself that I was certainly very open to making new friends, and invest in new friendships. It would be nice to have someone else to talk to and to share ideas with. I decided I might as well go out rather than spend another night alone at home. What's the worst that could happen? So, I drove there and I felt happy to see those three happy faces. Looking around, I realized that the other person was missing, or not there yet. My friend, being aware of what I was thinking, said that he was on his way. So, I thought, let's enjoy each other's company while we wait. Standing outside the pub, laughing at their jokes, I was trying to be part of the conversation but in reality, I was distracted and scanning every set of wheels that was driving by in the long parking lot through the misty, dimmed streetlights. There wasn't a lot of clarity to the imagination, but I also didn't have an idea of what I was checking for. My friend didn't describe the mystery guest to me. Did he look like Santa or Jack the Beanstalk? I had no idea what to look for, but that didn't last much longer. Shortly after I could see along the ground of the foggy, dark night, a set of steps walking towards us with a rhythm of determination and assertiveness. I got the feeling he was on a mission. I can never forget the deep sense of knowing that I knew the owner of those steps. The sense of familiarity was so real, like a dormant memory that had just awakened again. Only in a different reality and in a different time.

Curious eyes landed on me, to a certain extent, invading this memory that he too may have remembered but didn't know what to do with it. I couldn't hide from it, so I smiled and thought to myself: "wow, he does look like Santa," because of his handsome face filled with fur. Sweet, I thought to myself, he looks sweet, but oh my God, was he ever tall. And I couldn't help to think that he would be fine to be just a few inches shorter, and would still be very tall. But anyways, up in the air there was a beautiful kind of magic, filled with a strange comfort, that I believe, was awesome for all of us. In agreement with everyone, we went inside and decided to order dinner.

Great idea, and a beautiful tasty looking steak that never got eaten because the following 4 hours we were still gazing, talking and smiling. Oh yes, I forgot, that he was holding my hands, so I really couldn't feed myself. And because his hands were busy holding mine, he couldn't feed himself either. Oh yes, I need to share with you that he loved my red scarf. Perfectly laid around my neck and shoulders, revealing a slight bit of cleavage that I wasn't aware of, until I realized that he really had fallen in love with my scarf! And I can agree with him, I loved that red scarf too. That's why I bought it! Haha.

From there on it wasn't complicated, and certainly filled with a peaceful sense of truth and love. A kind of love that was safe, and that was willing to wait whatever time I needed. The third day after we met, he stopped by my work to see me and say hello. When he left, he left a key inside my hand, saying to me: "come home, I've been waiting for you all my life."

And then I thought: "sweet baby Jesus, and I've been waiting for you too!"

WITH ALL MY HEART AND LOVE, I COMPOSE

THE LEGEND OF THE KEY AND THE RETURN OF THE ROSE

(Excerpt from "My Rose Key" from Letters to God – my first book)

And that was my rose key, and the truth is, that I too had been looking for him. Since then, we have been always together and God knows that my love for him keeps on growing in ways that it will never have room to end.

TRUE LOVE IS A LANGUAGE THAT SAYS IT ALL WITHOUT SAYING A WORD.

The Challenging Sea of an Awoken Heart

Chapter 19

My Heart

Deep down in my heart I ask God that he grants us a few more years to enjoy life here on Earth, to work on the dreams that can bring us the freedom we never had, and to keep the peace we worked so hard for, to enjoy the children and the grandchildren in a way and a manner that is filled with appreciation and respect for them all, not forgetting and including us grandparents as we have walked the walk many times before. My husband is a wonderful man, and I cannot imagine my life without him, without his hold and his beautiful smile. He supports my dreams and encourages me to create everything that magnifies my heart and that helps me grow my wings. I know that regardless of whatever lays ahead we always have each other's back, and that our love is eternal and this is something that God and the universe will always support. I believe that they too recognized those steps, those steps I saw walking towards to me on the night that we first met; memories of many prints lived during different times long before.

Wow! What a journey filled with adventure, and at the same time challenged by destiny. I'm delighted that I've been chosen to live it and experience it all.

No, it's not "why me?" It's, "why not me?"

As I'm coming closer to the end of writing this book, I feel so blessed for having had so many opportunities of making choices, and for taking risks, even for believing in the people that didn't deserve my trust. I thank God, my Love, my Strength, and my Light, for having chosen me and for trusting me to get some beautiful work done and delivered to my fellow humans with love and compassion while I walk my walk.

Yes, God please stay by my side at all times! Please help me help everyone that seeks truth, seeks strength, but above all, everyone that seeks you, your light and your sacred heart.

Next, I'd like to share something that has just recently happened to me, and that has and will change the remainder of my life.

This was the beginning of August in 2024, when I was faced with an emergency with my heart. Yes, surprise! That is what I thought! But to a certain extent I've always known that the day would come. It was late at night when I started to feel extreme shortness of breath, and my heart beats were increasing rapidly. Oh, I was scared, and the more I tried to breathe, the harder my heart worked, so I decided to woke up my husband. I acted on it without any delay.

"Terry, honey, I need to go to the hospital," this was what I was saying while waking him up with gentleness and trying not to scare him too much. He opened his eyes and looked at me, he said" "oh okay, I will take you." He said it with some confusion, to which I replied: "no I need to call the ambulance, I believe I don't have enough time to be sitting in the emergency waiting room."

The Challenging Sea of an Awoken Heart

I really didn't, as every minute I was getting worse. The firefighters arrived quickly and the ambulance came shortly after. I was so happy to see them, but by then I was so sick that I honestly didn't think I was going to make it to the hospital. It was a good 20 minutes-drive away. I could see my husband's fear reflected in his eyes, but he was still staying positive and strong for me. The paramedics were awesome, and they treated me with love and kindness. They quickly got an IV going and gently loaded me into the ambulance to put me on oxygen. My heartbeat was up to 215 beats per minute. At some point the ambulance pulled over and another paramedic came in, and in truth I don't know exactly why but I believe that it was serious. How serious was their meeting I don't know, I couldn't hear what they were saying, however, part of me believes they were deciding whether or not to stop and restart my heart. In the end, they didn't, and after a short time the additional paramedic, which I believe was the supervisor, left and the ambulance continued speedily on route to the hospital. It felt like a short trip and I was still in extreme agony and struggling to breathe.

My husband was following the ambulance, and as soon we got there he was there too. I felt such gratitude to see him when the ambulance door opened at the Emergency doors at the hospital. As fast as the paramedics got me out of the ambulance and into the hospital, all kinds of emergency help arrived, and before I knew it, I was being moved to another bed and undressed and covered in a hospital gown. It felt good to have all the restrictive clothing removed, but the mortifying lack of oxygen was intense. The nurses were wanting me to lay down, but I kept on trying to sit up in order to get a breath. Then to be told to lay down again. The paramedics stood around for quite some time before leaving and wishing me well. To which I said thank you with a little wave goodbye. It was comforting to hear those words of kindness from the ambulance driver. She told me I was in good hands and would be well looked after.

Shortly after the doctor on duty came to visit and said: "Hi, I'm the doctor," and while looking at the heart monitor, he told me that I was going to be there for a very long time. I replied with a soft-spoken and humble "okay." I don't know how long it took to start feeling a little better but I know that I was able to breathe at some point, and immediately after I felt very sleepy. I was so extremely tired. At around 5AM in morning the cardiologist came to see me and said that he had ordered some tests and that in a few hours I'd be moved upstairs to CCU unit.

My poor husband was so tired. The last 4 turbulent hours really gave him a scare and a different perspective about life. I asked him to go home and try to get some rest. He asked if I was sure, not wanting to leave my side.

"Of course, I am," I replied, "you need to sleep and I'm going to try to get few minutes of it too."

After different tests and an ultra-sound, it was clear that my heart is in a weak condition, a heart-failure was the term the doctor used, and he said that it will need open heart surgery.

'Okay,' I thought, 'I already knew that, but I was hoping that it could be fixed by a smaller surgery.'

But oh well, I think I'm just going to stay in the gratitude that this isn't happening to my children, or my husband, or grandchildren, and for that I was, and am, in such deep appreciation. I'm happy to hear that my heart can be helped and healed. What a blessing I'm being presented with, another chance at life. God is looking after me!

I stayed in the hospital for a few days and continuously felt a little better every day. I loved my son's visit, and his love is always there filled with kindness and true care. My sisters also came to visit me, and we had some good laughs. The laughter helped lighten the energy and resonated with my true nature of being. I adored the simple, white hair brush that I asked for. It was my youngest sister and my niece who brought it to me the one evening when they were coming to visit. Three days in the hospital without having looked at myself, I realized my hair was so tangled, it felt like a fisherman's net.

The Challenging Sea of an Awoken Heart

Finally, the visit of my lovely friend Anieta, and the delicious blueberries that she brought in for me, wrapped up another beautiful day in my hospital bed.

I am home now and loving the feeling of being somewhat normal again. This heart failure and a ton of medications, as well as blood thinners, it's all certainly helping. However, a lot has changed and I am so thankful for being part of that change. A slower pace and more appreciation for every minute that I'm being gifted with to be here on Earth. During this entire life changing event, I feel in such peace knowing that the Lord is my shepherd, and that I'll always be looked after, or that He will lead me as He always has to look after myself.

With this book and my story coming to an end, I'd like to say that I am the mother of two beautiful children, they are pieces of my heart and filled my life with purpose and an unimaginable strength. Each gifted me with one precious grand-daughter. Both whom I love with all my being. Another daughter, that is my son's wife, and she too is my daughter, the one who is always there and I certainly love watching her evolving beautifully.

The blended family, another 4 children and 11 grandchildren, who too are very special for me, especially, the grandchildren, their pure love and appreciation for vavò's love.

My husband and my best friend, Terry is my rock, and I wouldn't want to see my life without him.

I live in British Columbia, in the City of Langley, and what a beautiful place to live. However, I'm thinking about Mexico, that beautiful ocean, palm trees and parrots. I want to teach them to speak Portuguese. Portuguese, Spanish, and Mexican are all very similar, so if those parrots are as smart as I think they are, they should be able to pick it up quickly. Haha. I'm just going to leave this wish in God's hands and see what happens. Who knows, it may be part of a future adventure.

The Challenging Sea of an Awoken Heart

Over the years I fully embraced the gift as I could no longer ignore the call of being chosen to do the work. To help people on both sides of the veil. I am a psychic Medium, a spiritual activist that loves communicating with passed-on people, and help healing ailments of past lives and of this life too. This is what I do full-time and worldwide. I am so blessed with so much love for the living and also for the dead, for I know death is life in a higher dimension of loving frequency, and it is that pure Love that has led my heart to never give up and has reminded me so often that there is still hope for humanity.

www.ingramcontent.com/pod-product-compliance
Lightning Source LLC
Chambersburg PA
CBHW062215080426
42734CB00010B/1893